Anne
Boleyn

For Steven Won Brannon, aged two, who has endured many hours of babysitters while his mother acted as chief critic and editor of this essay.

Praise for
Lacey Baldwin Smith

Henry VIII
'Witty and brilliant' *THE IRISH TIMES*
'A supremely satisfying book' *THE OBSERVER*
'The best book on Henry VIII that I have ever read... Smith brings the inner man alive for us in a way no other historian has done. The portrait is as convincing as it is compelling, absolutely authentic, marvelously readable.'
A. L. ROWSE

Treason in Tudor England
'A stunning evocation of a brutal age from one of our finest historians'
ALISON WEIR
'Any new book by Lacey Baldwin Smith is an event'
JOHN KENYON, *THE OBSERVER*

Catherine Howard
'Lacey Baldwin Smith has so excellently caught the atmosphere of the Tudor age' *THE OBSERVER*
'It is a measure of Smith's abilities as a historian that every word of what he writes seems true. The life of a noble household, the brawling city of London, and the colour and squalor of the Court glow in his pages, making a vivid background against which this pretty, feckless girl moves to her doom' J. H. PLUMB

TUK

Please return / renew by date shown.
You can renew at: **norlink.norfolk.gov.uk**
or by telephone: **0344 800 8006**
Please have your library card & PIN ready.

NORFOLK LIBRARY
AND INFORMATION SERVICE

NORFOLK ITEM

30129 070 061 859

Anne Boleyn

The Queen of Controversy
A Biographical Essay

LACEY BALDWIN SMITH

AMBERLEY

First published 2013

Amberley Publishing
The Hill, Stroud
Gloucestershire, GL5 4EP

www.amberley-books.com

British Library Cataloguing in Publication Data.
A catalogue record for this book is available from the British Library.

ISBN 978 1 4456 1023 8 (hardback)
ISBN 978 1 4456 1809 8 (ebook)

Typesetting and Origination by Amberley Publishing
Printed in Great Britain

Contents

Preface

The discerning reader might like to know why an eighty-nine-year-old man was silly enough to write yet another book on Anne Boleyn. Surely there are enough of them already. The answer resides in a telephone call I received from an English publisher with a heavy English accent which my defective hearing was quite incapable of understanding. So I turned the phone over to my daughter, in whose Washington DC house I was a four-month visitor escaping a northern Vermont winter. The first thing I heard was, 'That's a wonderful idea, I am sure he will be delighted.' The phone call was a passionate request for me to write a biography of Mistress Anne Boleyn. I had a year in which to do it, and it needed to be only 40–60,000 words. The brevity tempted me; I suspected my daughter's enthusiasm was partly the result of having me mope about the house with nothing to do; and I was tired of being treated like a precious antique. I suddenly realised that I not only had many of the source materials in my own library but I already knew a good deal about the subject. I had written a psychological biography of Henry VIII; a life-and-times account of the king's fifth wife, Catherine Howard; a short biography of Anne Boleyn's daughter, Elizabeth I; a social-psychological study of treason in Tudor England; and other books on the sixteenth century. So I said, 'Yes,' with the important proviso that the title should include the weasel phrase, 'A biographical essay.' The word 'essay' transforms both the form and the substance, allowing me to write without worrying about a full biographical discourse.

1
Setting the Stage

The story of Anne Boleyn goes to the root of all history: what makes an individual or event memorable to later generations? Anne is an exceptional case, for her life was a double helix intertwining extraordinary human drama with profound historical crisis. A young lady of no particular importance or talents – she was neither a great beauty nor a captivating charmer but possessed spectacular sex appeal – married a man who turned out to be England's most notorious monarch. Then three years later she was publicly executed for treason, accused of quadruple adultery, incest and conspiring to murder the king. While the human story is beyond the imagination of the most sensational Harlequin romance, the political script is as intriguing as a spy novel. At the same time Mistress Boleyn was the crucial catalyst for three of the most important events in modern history: the break with Rome causing the English Reformation, the advent of the nation state, and the birth of a daughter whose forty-three years on the throne stand as England's most spectacular literary and political success story. Remove Anne from the text of history and the English Reformation as we know it today would not have taken place; remove Anne and the timing of the nation state as it emerged in England would have been profoundly changed; remove Anne and Elizabeth I would not have existed at all. Anne Boleyn stands as a monument to the truth that there is nothing consistent in history except the unexpected.

Little wonder then that the second daughter of Sir Thomas Boleyn has attracted historians and novelists like bears to the honey pot. Optimistic scholars have laboured to bring verisimilitude and order to a life that lacks unbiased documentation only in the end to acknowledge their failure to make any sense out of her saga. Fiction writers, unrestrained by any obligation to prove their assertions, have assigned passions and motives that often ring true but for which there is not a scrap of historical evidence. Recently there are four new novels about Anne and two more are said to be forthcoming. She remains the most popular femme fatale, far outranking Cleopatra or Catherine the Great of Russia or even Bessie Wallis Simpson.

Anne may have been the divinely anointed Queen Consort of England for only 1,090 tumultuous days but she has reigned for the past 500 years as the undisputed queen of historical controversy. Her short time in her regal position was spectacular but what has made her drama exceptional and her brief stay on earth absolutely memorable has been the deluge of contradictions, confusion, doubts, biases and barefaced unknowns surrounding her life both as it was actually lived and as it has been told. It is probably no exaggeration to say that she had more ill-wishers, more unreliable sources, more prejudiced descriptions and analyses and fewer verifiable facts about her career than any woman, certainly any queen, since the beginning of recorded history. Anne Boleyn is the historian's perfect nightmare, a fascinating figure who remains, despite the most arduous labours of scholars, more fanciful than real, more fiction than verisimilitude.

For five centuries, debate and furore have prevailed about Anne's character, the circumstances of her life and the significance of her actions. Her own century had the most to say, although what passed for history was more highly slanted propaganda than objective truth. In the war over character assassination *versus* flattering acclaim the sides have lined up with no one seeking the middle ground of moderation or quest for truth. On the defamation side she was the source of all evil, the devil's disciple and a physical and spiritual monster; four names stand out: Eustace Chapuys, Nicholas Sander, Lancelot de Carles and George Cavendish. Chapuys was Emperor Charles V's ambassador to England almost continuously between 1529 and 1545 and his reports are the wellspring of 90 per cent of what we know about Anne. He detested her and never referred to her by name except as the 'concubine', 'the lady' or less frequently 'this devil of a concubine'. Sander, the Catholic polemicist, gathered together and published posthumously in 1585 the most scandalous stories he could find associated with Mistress Boleyn in his *The Rise and Growth of the Anglican Schism*, a popular Catholic best-seller. Carles was a minor factotum and poet in the French embassy in London who penned an epic verse-biography of Anne and her fall from grace within days of her execution. He admires her courage but not her morals. His *Histoire de Anne Boleyn Jadis Royne d'Angleterre* along with the imperial ambassador's reports are almost the only first-hand descriptions we possess. George Cavendish's biography of Cardinal Wolsey has much to say about Mistress Boleyn. Politically and religiously he was no friend of the lady. Why he makes her responsible for Cardinal Wolsey's fall from royal favour, accused of treason, is a mystery but he remains one of the few sources available for the story of Anne's life at court and early encounter with the king. Exactly how to use the information provided by these authors remains a matter of ferocious scholarly debate.

On the favourable side there are fewer names to pick from largely because praising Anne implied criticising Henry, a divine-right king who could do no wrong, and few sixteenth-century authors were willing to take the risk. The most stalwart defenders were John Foxe, the martyrologist, William Latimer, chaplain to Anne, and George Wyatt, amateur historian and unpublished biographer of the queen, all safely writing long after Henry VIII went to his grave. Foxe's eight-volume *Acts and Monuments*, better known as the *Book of Martyrs*, was once considered unreliable Protestant propaganda but today it is regarded as an indispensable source for the sixteenth century. His purpose, however, is transparent; he feels obliged to defend Anne's moral character and portray her as one of the principle founders of Protestantism in England as a way of influencing and pleasing queen Elizabeth, whom he urged to transform England into a Protestant paradise. William Latimer was one of the few biographers of the queen who actually knew her, and his *Cronickille* reveals the queen through Protestant rose-coloured glasses. George Wyatt was the grandson of Thomas Wyatt, one of the century's major poets, and the son of another Thomas Wyatt who led one of the more daring, if harebrained, political rebellions against Queen Mary in 1554. George Wyatt's purpose was to guard the morals of both Anne and his grandfather, who were accused of sleeping together, and save the queen from the scandalous reproaches of Nicholas Sander.

For the next 100 years history remained what it had always been, a moral lesson to display God's hand in determining the affairs of man: the good prevailing and the evil being punished. All of the biographical polemics on Anne belong in this category. By the mid-seventeenth century a change was taking place; history was becoming both humanised and secularised. The mind of God was being replaced by the mind of man, and Lord Herbert of Cherbury wrote the first 'modern' biography of Henry VIII, depicting the king as a unique human being, not the instrument of divine will. Anne appears in his portrayal without devil's horns or monstrous personality. Similarly in Bishop Gilbert Burnet's multi-volume history of the Reformation, originally written in 1679–81, Anne is presented as part of the complexities of the Reformation, not as a Protestant martyr or a devil besetting Catholicism.

The advent of the new secular history was the result of an intellectual revolution; the nineteenth-century explosion of interest in Anne Boleyn and her era was the product of a technological revolution. In the second half of the nineteenth century the historical holdings of the Public Record Office and the British Museum were catalogued and printed. For the first time researchers had at their disposal the *Calendar of State Papers Spanish* and *Venetian* and the massive *Letters and Papers of Henry VIII*. History was suddenly made far easier, scholars no longer had to ruin their eyes over illegible handwriting, precarious spelling and non-existent sentence structure; and equally important, history could be now replicated. The age of the footnote had dawned, and the quality and accuracy of an author's information could be authenticated.

Victorians were both fascinated and repulsed by the pathos and brutality of the sixteenth century. Anne emerges as the helpless and largely innocent victim of political lust and violence, although many Victorian writers had difficulty imagining a government plot against her because it was presumed that proper British statesmen simply did not behave that way. For most of these scholars, Anne's jury of her peers was pictured as worthy gentlemen and aristocrats who could have found Anne guilty only for good and sufficient reasons. Since the state offered little evidence against her, they resolved the problem by suggesting that most of the government's records proving her guilty had been either lost over the years or censored for sound political purposes.

Victorian historians were quarrelsome and prolific but the three who had the greatest influence in shaping Anne's historical reputation were James Anthony Froude, possibly the greatest of all Victorian historians, Paul Friedmann and Agnes Strickland. Froude parades nineteenth-century pride and virtue throughout his twelve-volume history of the British Isles between 1529 and 1588, which remains a classic and contains documentation found nowhere else except in the musty confusion of the archives. Agnes Strickland was the century's most vehemently romantic amateur historian, and she left an enduring image of Anne playing the innocent beauty to Henry VIII's monstrous beast. Alas, the kiss of marriage turned the beast not into a prince but her murderer. Paul Friedmann wrote the first full-length biography of the lady, in which he rarely has a complementary word to say about James Froude. His opinions, however, have withstood the test of time including his warnings that Eustace Chapuys's reports to his imperial master are dangerously biased and unreliable. Friedmann's biography of the lady reads as if it were a commentary on Ambassador Chapuys's dispatches, with lengthy footnotes quoting the original sixteenth-century French. The ambassador was a trained lawyer, a friend of the humanist Desiderius Erasmus, and an astute diplomat whose ears, in one modern biographer's words, 'became almost the confessional for the king's critics'.[1] Chapuys's pages are filled with truculent dislike for Anne and opposition to Henry's defiance of papal authority, and the nub of the question is whether or not to believe what he has left for history to judge. There are four places to read his words: the highly abbreviated translations in the *Letters and Papers of Henry VIII*, the fuller versions given in the *Calendar of State Papers Spanish*, Friedmann's French footnotes, and the enciphered original letters in the Haus-, Hof- und Staatsarchiv, Vienna. Professor G. W. Bernard displayed great academic one-upmanship as the only author to travel to Vienna and research the original reports, not that the effort reveals anything new. Friedmann is deeply negative about the future of research on Anne and concludes his biography by reiterating his pessimism: 'My object has been to show that very little is known of the events of those times, and that the history of Henry's first divorce and of the rise and fall of Anne Boleyn has still to be written.'[2]

Modern historians have been happy to take up Friedmann's challenge and write the definitive history of Anne's life and tribulations. Testing how successful they have been is the primary purpose of this essay. The year 2009, the 500th anniversary of Henry VIII's succession to the throne, has been the historical highlight for all current research on the Tudors, spawning a host of histories, novels, movies and television shows on Henry VIII, his six wives and his tumultuous century. Four modern scholars have recently responded to the immense popularity of the Tudor era and entered the fray of rewriting the saga of Anne Boleyn's life. Eric Ives, Emeritus Professor at Birmingham University, is the undisputed expert on Anne Boleyn. Unlike most historians he has had occasion to marshal and publish his views on Anne twice, first in 1986 under the title of *Anne Boleyn* and then again in 2004 as *The Life and Death of Anne Boleyn*, possibly not the most imaginative titles but, like his scholarship, impressively thorough. Professor G. W. Bernard of Southampton University has written a short biography of the queen that first took shape as a long article in the *English Historical Review*. His book bristles with controversy and turns the field on its head; alone among scholars he holds Anne Boleyn condemned as charged. Retha M. Warnicke, an American professor at the University of Arizona, was among the first of the four authors to publish her solution to the mystery and confusion surrounding Anne Boleyn's death. Her version came out in 1989 and has come under heavy attack, largely because her evidence stands alone and unsubstantiated like so many other interpretations of the queen's life. The final portrayal of Anne Boleyn was published in 2010 by Alison Weir, a professional writer, novelist and biographer, and is extraordinarily difficult to evaluate. On the surface it appears to be a perfectly respectable biography but since it deals with only the three and a half months surrounding her miscarriage and execution between late January and mid-May of 1536, it is unfair to compare it with other full-length accounts. More important and more worrisome, Weir's story is unverifiable since it has no acceptable footnotes. It dutifully cites sources but gives no page references. This produces a bizarre situation: the *Letters and Papers of Henry VIII* are referred to some 300 times but since there are a total of thirty-three volumes of these papers, any citation without pagination or volume numbers is worthless. One senses a great deal of research but there is no way to check it. The situation is rather like being asked to evaluate a fine piece of silver only to discover all the hallmarks have been obliterated with no way of determining the quality of the metal or the calibre of workmanship without melting down the entire work of art. Whether she should be compared to scholars with academic credentials is arguable but on the ground that some of history's greatest historians never used a footnote, there seems no good reason to exclude a biography of Anne that reads like a well-researched and delightfully written historical work.

My purpose in this biographical essay is not simply to evaluate modern scholarship on the queen of controversy but also to point out the manifold historiographical pitfalls that her life and tribulations entail and to reflect briefly on the emotional and intellectual atmosphere surrounding her accusation of adultery and high treason. One final question requires attention: why only four biographies under discussion? Weren't there others? There were, probably more than I am aware of, but if the truth were told, it is not always easy to differentiate a biography from a work of historical fiction. I have written a biographical essay, not a biography, and feel no great obligation to achieve total coverage on all fronts. Instead, I selected four studies that I felt were the best-researched, the best-written, developed the most interesting interpretations, and came closest to achieving something resembling historical truth.

2

Early Life & Education

It seems only appropriate that 'the queen of controversy' should have been born in the midst of historiographical debate: there is little agreement as to where or when she was born. Most children arrive in this world with a set of facts and figures attached; Anne has only two indisputably useful identifying features – she was a girl baby and a Boleyn baby. Having stated the two uncontroversial facts about Anne – her sex and her lineage – we are confronted with the muddle of much of the sixteenth century. Most people regard the era of Henry VIII as the dawn of modernity, the age of the Renaissance and Protestant Reformation, the absolute triumph of the lawyer, bureaucrat and Machiavellian analyst, and the birth of statistics and parish records kept not for reasons of the soul's welfare but as an act of state, the better to tax the body. Unfortunately, demographic details are almost as uncertain and unknown in the sixteenth century as in the medieval past. Neither the when nor the where of Anne Boleyn's birth are recorded with any certainty. The weight of modern scholarship strongly suggests she was born in Blickling, the Boleyn family residence in Norfolk just outside of Norwich, not Hever Castle in Kent, built by her great-grandfather Geoffrey Boleyn and Anne's acknowledged childhood home. Even more uncertain is the year of her birth. Two dates are offered. Until the 1980s the year *circa* 1507 was the accepted date. Today modern scholarship has opted for *circa* 1501, again with considerable emphasis on the *circa*. Professors Ives and Bernard accept the earlier dating; Professor Warnicke prefers the later 1507 birth year.[1]

Adding six years to Anne's age is important because it transforms her from a teenage ingénue of nineteen when she encountered the king into a mature woman of twenty-six. Equally important, it puts an end to the legend that Henry liked his ladies young. His first wife, Katherine of Aragon, was five and half years his senior, Anne Boleyn was thirty-one when married, Jane Seymour, his third spouse, was twenty-seven, Anne of Cleves was twenty-five, Catherine Parr was twice widowed before wedding Henry at thirty-one and Catherine Howard, the fifth wife and youngest, was probably twenty-two. Moreover, assigning the first year of the century as Anne's natal year pushes her back into the medieval twilight. She emerged a Renaissance lady but her tutors were the product of the medieval past.

There is general consensus about Anne Boleyn's early life: nothing is known about it. Her great-grandfather,

Geoffrey Boleyn, was the start of the family's rise to aristocratic status. He was in trade, probably the wool trade, and acquired the financial wherewithal to leave Norfolk in the 1420s and settle in London, rise to become a city alderman and Lord Mayor, and marry the daughter of Thomas, Lord Hoo. His son William furthered the process, marrying into the peerage, this time the Butler family of the Irish Earls of Ormonde, and settling down as a landed country gentleman with a knighthood in 1483. The third generation, Anne's father Thomas, moved into the political big time, marrying Elizabeth, the eldest daughter of Thomas Howard, Earl of Surrey, soon to become the Duke of Norfolk and leader of the aristocratic old guard at court. Thomas Howard's father had been Duke of Norfolk under Richard III and both father and son fought on the losing side at the Battle of Bosworth Field that assured the crown to the Tudors. The father died in battle, the son spent three years in the tower until he made his devotion to the new king clear; his loyalty was to the crown, whoever might be wearing it, not to the fallen Yorkist monarchy. Eventually he became Henry VIII's most important military workhorse, and when the king was off fighting chivalric battles in France, it was the Earl of Surrey who triumphed over the Scots at the Battle of Flodden in 1513, where 10,000 Scots and their king fell in battle. In reward Surrey regained his father's title of Duke of Norfolk. He stood as something of a medieval relic, but until his death in 1524 he was one of England's premier noblemen.

Thomas Boleyn could not help but profit from his marriage into the Howard clan, and he soon became a skilled diplomat and royal councillor and eventually Treasurer of the king's household, a crucial position giving him access to the king's person, but it was his daughter Anne who managed for him the noble titles of Earl of Wiltshire and Earl of Ormonde. Thomas has, however, suffered over time as the victim of the courtier stereotype, embodying all of the evils, discomforts and corruptions of court, a gilded misery of 'pride, envy, indignation, and mocking, scorning and derision'. He would, it was said, 'sooner act from interest than from any other motive'. The truth of that statement was tested when he served on the commission of inquiry, much like a modern-day Grand Jury, which unanimously accused his daughter and son of adultery, incest and high treason. What Anne's father was really like is lost in time. Whether she received affection or attention from an ambitious parent who was either on diplomatic mission or at court much of the time is pure speculation.

Her mother, Elizabeth Howard, is nothing but a name in history, possibly of great emotional influence but totally undocumented. An unlikely rumour adheres to her name: one of the wilder Catholic polemicists accused her of having slept with the king, and that Henry VIII was actually Anne's father. Elizabeth filled the nursery at Hever Castle with three children and at least two others died young. Anne's birth in 1501 is reasonably well attested and Eric Ives has cause to think that Mary was a year older, and George somewhat younger than his sisters.[2] But like almost everything about the Boleyns, anything as precise as a birth date is little more than speculation and guesswork. Mary was not only a year older but also may have been better-looking, which led to her becoming the king's mistress, but being by far the less vivacious, intelligent and charismatic of the two she commanded Henry's bed for only a short time. One thing, however, can be said with certainty; the Boleyns gave Anne an excellent education. We know this not from the process but through the results: Anne not only expressed herself with loquacious grace but was fluent in French, so much so that she became a valuable tool to her father's diplomatic manoeuvrings. She read with discernment the latest books on religion and politics. No historian has anything to say about Anne's educational upbringing for the excellent reason there is no documentation, only the conclusion that she must have had extensive training. Although the names of her tutors and the range of her curriculum are unknown, we do possess a fair knowledge of the general outlines and aims of early sixteenth-century schooling, which are worth recounting.

1. The king's lock-plate, similar to that found in Hever Castle. When Henry visited a private home he had his carpenters install special locks on the doors of his bedchamber and living quarters.

Had Anne been a boy she might have gone to petty and then to grammar or high school; both were becoming popular in the early sixteenth century. A son would have been exposed to a rigid and well-thought-out curriculum designed to turn corrupt and unruly children into loyal and dutiful subjects of the crown, and supply them with enough social graces and mastery of Latin to allow them to pass themselves off as gentlemen. Daughters were not barred from petty school, but grammar school was the exclusive domain of the male, and Anne would have had to complete her training at home. Most likely, however, a young girl of Anne's social standing was totally schooled at home, and what she learned was a reflection of the interests and competence of her tutors and the influence of her parents. In most families it was not deemed necessary to train girls in rhetoric, poetry or the Classics; it was considered sufficient if they could read, write and embroider. Given the final product, it is clear that Anne was trained in far more than the feminine graces and needlework. In all probability she had a full masculine education, which started out as purely religious, then graduated into English and Latin grammar, and ended up with the classical authors and a heavy emphasis on rhetoric and decorum, of which there were two kinds: how to structure your thinking and writing so that means and ends were always in accord with one another, and how to move gracefully in that level of society assigned you by God.

At its most rudimentary, Tudor education had little to do with reading and writing and everything to do with rote memory and instilling young minds with the basic tenets of the Christian creed. Four- and five-year-olds were expected to memorise the Ten Commandments, the twelve articles of the Apostles, and the Lord's Prayer because 'he that understandeth these three hath the pythe of all those things which Holy Scripture doth contain'.[3] Since printed grammar books did not begin to appear until the mid-century mark, reading and writing relied almost entirely on the Bible, especially the Book of Proverbs and Ecclesiasticus, often called the Wisdom of Sirach. Ecclesiasticus no longer appears in the Protestant Bible but in the sixteenth century it was an integral part of Scriptures and the central text in a child's education. Sirach's wisdom had little to do with religion per se and everything with surviving in a dangerous and difficult world. It was the Tudor era's 'advice book' of choice.

Anne Boleyn would have read Ecclesiasticus in English, translated it into Latin and back again into the vernacular, and listened to it on a daily basis at lunch and dinner. Sirach starts with the accepted universal truth that 'all wisdom cometh of God', and quickly goes on to exhort his young readers in what was the central tenet of family existence: 'Listen to me, your father, my children, and act in such away that you may be preserved. For the Lord has glorified the father above his children, and he has established the rights of the mother over her sons... Honor your father in word and deed so that his blessing may attend you.' Having pronounced the truth of family life he spends the bulk of his text on how to survive in a friendless and deceiving world and how to act with decorum and respect to one's betters, listing the cardinal don'ts of good manners: don't belch near a man's face, don't scratch your head at meal time, don't blow your nose on your napkin, don't break wind in public, and don't 'look at what comes out of your nose'.

Most of Sirach's time is given to cautioning the child what to expect in later life, and his book is filled with dire admonitions about the frailty of friendship. 'If thou getteth a friend, prove him fast and be not hastied to give him credence.' Over and over he warns that 'there are some friends that turneth to enemitie' and he begs youth to 'depart from your enemies, yea, and beware of your friends'. Life is filled with snares and deceptions, and for 136 pages (by far the longest book in the apocrypha) Ecclesiasticus offers excellent advice: 'lend not unto him that is mightier than thyself, if thou lendeth him count it but lost'; go 'not to law with a judge'; and 'bring not every man into thine house, for the deceitful layeth in wait diversely'. Never 'trust thine enemy', for he has 'sweet in his lips' and speaks many good things and 'can weep with his eyes but in his heart he imagineth how to throw thee into a pit' and 'cannot get blood enough'. Do 'not take counsel with a fool, for he will not be able to keep the matter secret', and 'do not do a secret thing before a stranger, for you do not know what he will bring forth'. Do not 'forsake an old friend, for a new one is not equal to him. A new friend is new wine; when it grows old, you will enjoy drinking it'. And finally, 'keep far from a man who has the power of life and death... If you do approach him, do not offend him so that he may not take away your life. Understand that you are striding along among traps and walking on the city battlements', a warning that Anne Boleyn would have done well to heed.[4]

Respect for one's parents and proper etiquette along with a thorough knowledge of Latin started young in Tudor

England. Older children, seven to ten years of age, were exposed to Cato's verses and Aesop Fables, both edited and collected by Erasmus. Then followed three years of Cicero and close attention to rhetoric, the ability of the mind to 'handle any cause called in contention that may through reason largely be discussed'.[5] Cicero was the gospel from which stemmed all rhetorical knowledge, and his Latin prose was the model for all to emulate, especially his *copia* or copiousness, the art of illustrating any subject with a multitude of examples. Students were encouraged to keep commonplace books filled with apt saying, examples, comparisons, similarities and opposites to be used in their future themes and discourses. If there is a single difference between sixteenth-century and modern writing habits and concepts of literary organisation it has to do with *copia*; five examples were always considered better than two. In the hands of a Shakespeare or Marlowe copiousness produced the marvellous magic of a rich and varied style; in the hands of the average person it generated repetition, long-windedness, dullness and pure tedium. In chapter 6 the reader will encounter a heavy dose of *copia* in the form of Tudor constitutional legalese.

Composition writing not only organised the mind, it also taught decorum that was regarded as being next to piety, the cardinal goal of the educational process. Decorum or comeliness, fitness and decency was the knowledge of what was proper in relationship to 'the thing said or done, the

end in view, the persons involved, the time and the place'.[6]
No educational ideal has ever been so optimistic in what
it demanded of young minds, for decorum assumed that
a suitable and learned response was available for every
situation, and that it was possible for students to catalogue,
recite and apply the mandate. Since Anne left no diary, no
journal, almost no letters, and no school work it is impossible
to say to what extent her tutors successfully exposed her to
rhetoric and decorum, which were only just becoming the
essential core of Tudor education when Anne was in the
schoolroom. Whether new educational ideas trickled down
from London to the Boleyn country estate at Hever Castle
in Kent is hard to say, except that her father, Sir Thomas,
was clearly an educated man, fluent in French, and being at
court he must have been aware of the newest Renaissance
curriculum. Anne's mastery of social decorum is easier
to record for it was acquired during the teens, anywhere
between thirteen and sixteen, when children left home and
the schoolroom for final educational finishing in the homes
of the rich and mighty, in Anne's case as a lady-in-waiting
within the household of Margaret, Regent and Archduchess
of Burgundy.

The trip to Burgundy is documented by two letters, one from
the Regent to Sir Thomas Boleyn for the first time mentioning
and actually describing Anne, the other a short note from Anne
herself to her father revealing that she was perfectly aware
why she had been packed off to Europe. The previous year

Sir Thomas had been the English ambassador to the court of the archduchess, and had persuaded her to accept his daughter Anne as one of her eighteen *fille d'honneur*. After Anne arrived at the regent's court at Malines, located in northern Belgium close to Brussels, Margaret wrote Anne's father and for the first time lifted the veil of documentary silence that had surrounded her. 'I find,' she penned, 'her so bright and pleasant for her young age that I am more beholden to you for sending her to me than you are to me.'[7] Anne was thirteen give or take a few months, and this is the first hint of the woman she would become. The second letter is undated and written some time after the archduchess's note. In it Anne appears as the model child of her century, dutiful, obedient and assuring her father she wanted only what he desired for her, to be 'a woman of good reputation'. When she returned to England she looked forward to having mastered French so that she could speak with ease to the king's 'wise and virtuous' wife, Katherine of Aragon, and become one of the queen's ladies-in-waiting. This she desired 'because you have told me to, and have advised me for my own part to work at it as much as I can'.[8]

At Malines, Anne found herself at the finishing school for kings and queens and the aristocratic elite of Europe. The Duchy of Burgundy was a medieval leftover, bits and pieces of it sprawled over Western Europe between France and Germany. Today it includes most of Holland and Belgium. The duchy was slowly giving way to the encroachment of the nation state but the regent's court was still the cultural hub of

Northern Europe. It housed and schooled Margaret's thirteen-year-old nephew, Charles, Duke of Burgundy, the future Holy Roman Emperor and King of Spain, as well as his sisters and the many children of the aspiring nobility of England and the Continent. In all likelihood Anne's schoolroom education was over although Erasmus's educational text, *De Copia*, had just been published the year before she arrived and was rapidly becoming the predigested source from which all educated people acquired their knowledge of rhetoric and copiousness. The 1512 edition of his text had 818 entries of quotable examples of copiousness; by the 1540 edition that number had swollen to 3,260 so popular and useful the book had become. What for Anne Boleyn had just begun was schooling in being a proper lady, in other words role-playing. This entailed above all else training in deportment and proper decorum, which meant that Anne learned not merely fluent French with a private tutor, but also the latest dances and court etiquette. Masques, balls, and banquets were important events of the day and young girls not only had to wait on the archduchess but also perform in court rituals. Her talents seem to have run to languages and music, and even her detractors later admitted that Mistress Boleyn 'perfectly knew how to sing and dance' and 'play the lute and other instruments'.

The archduchess's court was like any other schoolroom environment, carefully chaperoned and protected from the taint of sexual scandal and the advances of young pages and ushers with lustful eyes for pretty young *filles d'honneur*. The records contain few hints of sexual skirmishes, only the tedium of good breeding and excellent taste in art, literature and fine needlework. Anne was introduced to the great Flemish painters, especially Hieronymus Bosch, Pieter Brueghel and Jan Van Eyck, and the exquisite illuminations of the Lowlands, the Duke of Berry's *Book of Hours* among them. The days and months passed by in 'the inaudible and noiseless foot of time' as Anne learned her allotted role in life. She did so, however, with no dates, records or stories to sustain and document the historian's imagination. The occasional letter that Anne has left us to read, mostly thank-you notes, would indicate that she was a firm believer in copiousness, indulged excessively in the run-on sentence and seems to have benefited little from the rigid ground rules of both intellectual and social decorum – a proper relationship between the end desired and the means utilised.

3
Cultural & Religious Environment

If we cannot describe the exact content of Anne's schooling, we can state with considerable confidence the ultimate aim of Tudor pedagogical instruction that was universal, although male oriented in most aspects: 'to catechise him in religion truly, frame him in opinion rightly, fashion him in behaviour civilly'.[1] Possibly a fourth category should be added: train him in comprehension thoroughly. Formal education constituted only a small fraction of the educational process that sought to shape sixteenth-century sensibilities and did not require literacy to absorb the assumptions, prejudices and associations that underlay the mental structure of Anne's society. Such a definition far exceeded the schoolroom and the tutor; it encompassed the total indoctrination and impregnation of young imaginations, how they understood the universe and God's purpose, how they responded to the mystery of existence, and how they determined cause and effect as men and women interacted with one another. These were essential concepts that every child was expected to chew, digest and convert 'into the substance of the mind'. Anne's biographers have little to say about shaping a child's consciousness because again this requires a vast amount of undocumented speculation. What the child learns either in the classroom or from the dogma of daily life eventually shapes the adult, determining our styles of thinking and our perceptions of the events around us. They may have had little immediate effect on the humdrum of Anne's daily life but are vital in establishing the mental stage on which her courtship, marriage, and ultimate execution took place, and in understanding the operation of minds profoundly different from our own.

Since Anne would eventually marry a divine-right monarch, her life touched more intimately than most upon the sixteenth-century comprehension of the universe. She inherited a cosmos that was God's miraculous handiwork.[2] Out of the chaos of unformed matter the deity had forged a harmonious and rational totality that was interconnected, hierarchical and infused with moral purpose. There was a place for everything from the most insignificant glob of matter to the most sublime seraph guarding the throne of the heavenly sovereign. All creation was linked in an endless chain of being that assured to the universe a tripartite unity – spiritual, physical and moral. There was throughout God's cosmos the rule of 'degree, priority and place', and the four orders of creation – animal, vegetable, mineral and the invisible, angelic spiritual inhabitants of the heavenly spheres. All was ordered according to its inherent worth or nobility and closeness to the deity. The lion held the chief place in the animal kingdom, as did the king in the human world. The eagle was prince of the skies, the oak stood first among trees, and the diamond was the most valued of gems.

2. The title page of Robert Fludd's *Tomus Secundus de Supernaturali, Naturali, Praeternaturali Microcosmi Historia* depicting the Tudor cosmos. Man is shown at the centre of the universe with the four earthly elements – fire (cholera), air (*sanguis*), water (pituita) and earth as the centre of the sphere. Outside the domain of man rotate the spheres of the heavenly hierarchy, angels through seraphim. God the creator is represented as a blast of light at the top and outside of the final circle.

Shakespeare penned the most famous statement of Tudor belief in cosmic order extending from the vaults of heaven to the domain of man when he wrote,

How could communities
Degree in schools and brotherhoods in cities,
Peaceful commerce from dividable shores,
The primogenitive and due of birth
Prerogative of age, crowns sceptres laurels,
But by degree stand in authentic place?
Take but degree away, untune that string,
And hark, what discord follows...[3]

More contemporary to Anne's generation are the words of the educator Thomas Elyot in his *Book named the Governor*:

Hath not God set degrees and estates in all his glorious works? First in his heavenly ministers, [angles] whom he hath constituted in divers degrees called hierarchies ... Behold also the order that God hath put generally in all his creatures, beginning at the most inferior or base and ascending upward ... Every kind of trees, herbs, birds, beasts and fishes have a peculiar disposition appropered unto them by God their creator; so that in everything is order, and without order may be nothing stable or permanent.[4]

The doctrine of primacy of place linked the Tudor cosmos into a satisfying and comprehensible vertical totality while a series of interlocking 'correspondences' or similarities knitted it together horizontally, supplying Anne and her contemporaries with their most distinctive frame of reference and habit of mind. The structure of thought that organised perceptions and occurrences as sympathetic associations or correspondences between events and ideas, which in most cases the twenty-first century would dismiss as nonsensical and bearing no relationship to one another, was an essential cultural heritage stemming from the medieval past and was universal to the Tudor age. From Sir Thomas More to Francis Bacon, the Tudors instinctively tended to see 'similarities more readily than it did differences', and postulate a system of correspondences between the perfection of God's domain and the material corruption of man's world. As Francis Bacon put it, 'nothing can be found in the material globe which has not its correspondence in the crystalline'.

An intimate relationship existed between the macrocosm of God's creation and the microcosm of the human body. Rivers and natural waterways corresponded to the bloodstream, air was analogous to breath, God's law was comparable to human reason, and cosmic and social disorder corresponded to man's anger and passion. Thomas Elyot dignified and elevated his role as an educator by claiming a triple correspondence between angels, the elements, and man: 'And like as the angels which be most in contemplation be highest exalted in glory ... and also the fire which is the most pure of elements is deputed to the highest sphere or place; so in this world they which excel other in this influence of understanding and do employ it to the detaining of others within the bounds of reason and show them how to provide for their necessary living, such ought to be set in a more high place than the residue, where they may see and also be seen.'[5]

The most common and popular correspondence in the sixteenth century was between the human body and political institutions – the body politic. Thomas Starkey, Henry VIII's chaplain and contemporary of Thomas Cromwell, a street-smart and low-born legal adviser to Cardinal Wolsey and member of parliament, depicted in his *Dialogue Between Cardinal Pole and Thomas Lupset* the Tudor commonweal as a human organism in all its artistic glory.

Like as in every man there is a body and also a soul in whose flourishing and prosperous state both together standeth the weal and felicity of man; so likewise there is in every commonalty, city and country as it were a politic body and another thing also resembling the soul of man, in whose flourishing both together resteth also the true common weal. This body is nothing else but the multitude of people, the number of citizens in every commonalty, city or country...

For like as all wit, reason and sense, springeth out of the heart, so from the princes and rulers of the state cometh all laws and policy, all justice, virtue and honesty to the rest of this politic body ... To the arms are resembled both craftsmen and warriors which defend the rest of the body from injury of enemies outward and work and make things necessary to the same; to the feet the ploughmen and tillers of the ground, because they by their labour sustain and support the rest of the body.[6]

Correspondences were far more than literary metaphors, they were descriptions of reality, and wherever one turns in the sixteenth century the doctrine of correspondence appears. Tudor sumptuary legislation, whereby clothing was prescribed for different estates in society, was based upon the assumption of a link between who you were and what you wore. The same was true in the medical profession; there was a clear association between outward appearance – colour and complexion – and inner temperament: sanguine, melancholic, choleric. The kernel of the walnut looked like the human brain in miniature, and therefore it made perfect medicine for headaches and head wounds. Lord Hungerford was executed for high treason in 1540 because of the correspondence between buggery, an unnatural act, and treason, a universal perversity. As we shall see the doctrine played a vital and fatal role in Anne Boleyn's trial for adultery and treason. It was a certainty, as William Baldwin put it, that 'the outward things which the eye of man only beholdeth are but weak and uncertain tokens of the inward secrets'.

The cosmos had been made in God's image and as a consequence it buzzed with moral meaning and the presence of an extraordinary number of interfering agents who inhabited God's heavenly mansion. Both God and Satan were activists who did not sit idle speculating. They both interposed and interfered and imbued all events with moral and historic meaning. When Thomas Cranmer went on diplomatic mission to Germany in 1532 he was confronted with a magnificent interplanetary display that was described as a flaming sword and horse's head in the sky. 'What strange things these token do signify to come hereafter' he did not know but he was quite sure they only occurred 'against some great mutation'.[7] Between 1506 and 1533 comets and eclipses appeared 'after which followed many and strange effects' ranging from sweating sickness in England and the death of Emperor Maximilian to Henry VIII's divorce 'from his brother's wife'. Not only did astral commotion correspond to human calamities, successes and deaths but God could also strike directly from heaven. Men were destroyed, maimed or sickened by avenging enemies, wild animals and disease, and bells and church-towers were forever being struck down by Satan. God 'beareth the kiss of life and death' for 'nothing happeneth without Him which is the first and principle mover, either for health or sickness, prosperity or adversity, riches or poverty'.[8]

3. This drawing shows the cathedral before lightning struck the steeple, one of the tallest in Europe, burning away the top of the tower in 1561. The building was destroyed in the Great Fire of London in 1666 which destroyed two-thirds of the city, and was replaced by Christopher Wren's magnificent monument to Renaissance architecture in the early eigtheenth century.

Divine providence was ubiquitous and absolute, and nothing differentiates the twenty-first century from the sixteenth more than today's willingness to view coincidence and chance as perfectly acceptable relationships between events. In Tudor England and all of Europe men searched for similarities in all things, and in a teleological universe where God played a dynamic role, coincidence was impossible. As William Baldwin later in the century urged, 'Search for everything,' by which he meant not modern scientific research into what can be isolated and controlled but quite literally, search for 'the cause of everything'.[9] Men and women even today are suspicious of coincidence, not just detectives and sleuths, for too much coincidence undermines our ability and need to impose rational order on the universe and control the chaos we sense exists just over the horizon. We prefer causal relationships and we hesitate to dismiss accidental events as meaningless occurrences. If a house owner steps out the front door onto a banana peel, falls and breaks his leg, two questions immediately leap to mind: why did the banana peel happen to be in his path, and what had the owner done to deserve such an unpleasant fate? The possibility that neither question is answerable and that there is no causal relation between the accidental placement of the peel and the person who stepped on it, other than the coincidental overlapping of two separate happenings in time and place, is alien to those of us who require purpose and unity in our lives. Either someone was bent upon harming the house owner and had deliberately arranged the location, or God had permitted the peel to be situated at the doorstep to punish the owner because of some moral defect. If today's analyst is open on the debate, Anne Boleyn and her generation were perfectly clear about the answer. They insisted that every natural disaster had to have a moral origin. Even the accidental revelation of Anne's own misbehaviour had to be God's will. The use of such terms as chance, fortune and coincidence 'proceeded first of ignorance and want of true knowledge, not considering what God is, and by whose only foresight and providence, all things in the world are seen of Him before they come to pass'.[10] Chance in the sixteenth century was nothing but an outward appearance, the result of failing to discover 'the cause of everything'. A case in point was the Tudor government's strenuous and paranoid efforts to track down the sources of evil and dangerous rumours. Today we regard rumours as the spontaneous work of many tongues by which a story is improved by the telling. The sixteenth century insisted that an evil rumour had to be the product of an evil person who had to be found and punished.

Standing behind moral cohesion and divine accountability was the paradoxical position of man in God's cosmos. He was the heaven-descended master on earth, a 'marvellous and cunning piece of work' and 'the head and chief of all that ever God wrought' yet he was 'nuzzled in sin' and his residence on earth was as far from heaven as it is possible to get. His abode was the curse of a double fall: Lucifer beset by insatiable pride had been cast out of heaven and ordered to live in hell, a close neighbour to the centre of the earth; Adam and Eve had been evicted from paradise because they had listened to the temptations offered by the devil and eaten of the tree of knowledge. Thus they were imprisoned in that sink of corruption, death, suffering and mutability called earth.

Devoid though he was of virtue and beatitude, man nevertheless held the critical place in the great chain of existence. He was absolutely unique, for he alone supplied the crucial bridge between the lower material and animal levels and the higher spiritual rungs that culminated in the throne of God. Man possessed the gift, and therefore the responsibility, of free choice to do either right or wrong, and alone in the universe he was endowed with the miracle of birth. Angelic citizens of God's spiritual domain were without sex; only within the cesspool of earth were new souls created which could be claimed by God or Satan and over whom the forces of good and evil struggled. As Francis Bacon described the situation, if man 'were taken away ... the rest would seem to be all astray, without aim or purpose ... and leading to nothing'.[11]

Closely allied to this egocentric view of the universe was the anthropomorphic conviction that both heaven and hell conformed to the rules and standards of human society. Angels existed 'in marvellous and inconceivable numbers because the honour of a king consists in the great multitude of his vassals and his disgrace or shame in their paucity'.[12] As for the devil's domain, it was a perversion and distortion of all that was good and loyal on earth. Much of the intensity of feelings and emotionalism of the period was related to this animistic and anthropomorphic approach to existence, in which virtue and vice were endowed with human features. There is, commented Clifford Gertz, an 'ingenerate tendency of men to anthropomorphise power', and throughout the sixteenth century war and the functions of state were dressed in a human guise that could be directly visualised and described.[13] War was not an impersonal conflict between insensate social systems but a clash of heroes and villains encouraged or soothed by such animate ideals as virtue, honour, courage and justice or hatred and evil. Diplomacy was viewed less as a balancing act between political and economic goals as a dynastic and chivalric struggle between right and wrong. Governmental authority without human features and personal responsibility was almost unimaginable. Few men would have dared to accept the challenge of the vicar of Ticehurst who, when pointing to an image of Henry VIII, asked, 'How darest thou spit upon this face? Thou darest not do it...'[14]

Of all of the afflictions that beset the Tudor period, the presence of the devil with his unholy gang of vices and kingdom of demonic agents was the most active, threatening at times to replace God Himself as the prime mover on earth. His purpose was to purchase souls for hell and to destroy all unity and loyalty, all love and government by sowing the seeds of discord and exercising the tools of his trade – dissimulation, seduction and intrigue. Satan was the 'father of liars and the chief author of deceit'. He stalked the land leaving in his wake sickness, failure, sterility, bankruptcy and death. The devil seemed to be on the rampage; the violence and brutality surrounding the religious strife of the Reformation providing terrifying proof of his existence. The reality of evil as a corporal and militant entity was as fundamental to Tudor England as the 'million of spiritual creatures' that everybody knew walked 'the earth unseen, both when we wake and when we sleep'. It was an instinctive reaction to look for and to discover evil in whatever shape it cared to assume.[15]

Sixteenth-century advice literature, especially the Wisdom of Sirach, was obsessed with the existence of evil and the intrigues of malicious people, and it offered detailed guidance on how to subvert the machinations of the wicked, unravel their plots and distinguish the true from the false, the real friend from the feigned. Invariably, the enemy was not just an adversary; he was also a villain replete with a recognisable face or more accurately a mask behind which he operated. As a consequence, the enemy might be anywhere: among one's personal friends, in the midst of one's household, or in the anteroom of the king's privy chamber. No one was immured from his potential enemy. The indoctrinated state of mind that evil was ubiquitous and hid behind hypocrisy, fakery and dissimulation gave to political life, and the operation of rival factions at court, a tension and intensity mitigated in the twenty-first century by the existence of muted, faceless and often amoral systems. For Anne Boleyn's age the most trivial and innocent remark, when taken out of content, could be construed as a grand design of infamy; the fear that fakery and ill will were the natural order of the world was universal. Evil by definition always possessed human features; it was a social and intellectual reflex that every form of malcontent, be it heresy, treason or economic malfeasance, was the result of personal evil. Such a response to life's calamities was inherent in the mental habit that assumed the existence of the interconnectedness of all things – buggery and treason, maledictions and bad luck, wax images pierced with pins and political assassinations, dreams of the loss of a tooth and the death of a friend, the birth of Siamese twins and the death of kings, and 'a blazing star' and Henry VIII's annulment of his marriage to Katherine of Aragon and the break with Rome.

Great astral commotion, it was said, foretold Henry's jettisoning of his first wife but the heavens were singularly silent when in 1513 Anne Boleyn made the all-important trip from her English home at Hever Castle to the palace of Archduchess Margaret of Austria, Regent of Burgundy. The only sense of external change that reached in to touch Anne's life was the dynastic whimsy of Tudor diplomacy as Cardinal Wolsey and his royal master Henry VIII wavered between the two European diplomatic poles of Valois France and the Habsburg family interests in Burgundy, Spain, Austria and the Holy Roman Empire. England's commitment to Burgundy and the imperial interests went far back in time and was predicated on English wool having free entry to Europe though the Lowlands and the historic enmity between England and France, the two kingdoms having been at war as long as anyone could remember. Wolsey and his sovereign not only continued the old alliance favouring the Habsburg interests but also tried to act as the fulcrum between France and growing Habsburg political and military power. The chimeric King Hal, however, did introduce one new element: he wanted to end his father's parsimonious neutrality and join in on the game of international armed conflict in which the dramatic, magnificent and chivalric carried more weight than the practical or the profitable. He was, as he publicly proclaimed, 'not unmindful that it was his duty to seek fame by military skill' and 'create such a fine opinion about his valour among all men that they would clearly understand that his ambition was not merely to equal but indeed to excel the glorious deeds of his ancestors'.[16] Henry was always a little long-winded, but within two years of his father's death in 1509 he was at war with France.

The king, however, was at a severe disadvantage in the international sport of kings in which Italy, with her enviable wealth from trade and banking, her rich culture and her papal states, was the coveted objective. England was far inferior to France in wealth and population and was crippled in any war with its channel neighbour lest Scotland invade through the back door. The essence of great power diplomacy was summed up by Francis I when he assured Henry that 'a King of France will never suffer a King of Scotland to be oppressed' any more 'than a King of England will suffer an emperor or a King of France to be overcome one of another', but will 'keep them in an equality'.[17] Moreover, the island kingdom was far removed from the central attraction of Venice, Milan, Naples and the Vatican seat at Rome. France and the Habsburgs could send armies to plunder or purchase the art and luxury of the Renaissance but Henry had to settle for chivalric excursions into France to plague his brother monarch and on occasion bankroll his allies. By 1513 he had won a skirmish in France but the Earl of Surrey with the king's wife, Katherine of Aragon, acting as regent in his absence, had achieved a far greater military triumph at Flodden Field against the Scots. Henry was not pleased.

A startling change of allies and enemies in 1514 led Henry to renege on his long-standing promise to marry his sister Mary to Archduke Charles of Burgundy, heir to the crowns of Austria and the Spanish kingdoms of Aragon and Castile, which went back to before his father's death. Instead his sister was suddenly married off to the widowed and rickety King Louis XII of France. It was the result of this diplomatic revolution that precipitated Anne's moving from the Burgundy court to Paris as a lady-in-waiting for Mary Tudor. There is no clear evidence that Anne attended the royal wedding at Abbeville despite her useful fluency in French, but she did turn up in Paris for the Coronation, a crown that survived only for eighty-two days for Louis died, aged fifty-two, leaving Mary a widow at eighteen and his grandson Francis I itching to prove his chivalric valour by continuing the never-ending war with the Habsburgs.

With the widowed Mary Tudor waiting to be returned to England, what was going to happen to her entourage, of which Anne was a part? Mysteriously Anne stayed on in Paris in the service of Claude, the wife of the new King of France and herself the daughter of Louis XII by a second marriage and now queen in her own right. None of Anne's biographers have an answer to her close ties to Claude except to surmise that the French queen took a liking to the young English girl when she was attached to Mary Tudor's household. Anne remained in France for another six years, which were filled with ritual and decorum surrounding a malformed queen who suffered from scoliosis, was pregnant most of the time, and did not join in the sexual escapades and excesses of her husband's 'privy band of ladies'. Though Anne's later enemies did their best, there is no evidence that Anne acquired in France a reputation similar to that of her sister Mary, who also spent a brief period in Paris on Mary Tudor's court, as a 'great wanton and notoriously infamous' woman. Claude seems to have been as strict and virtuous as Margaret, Archduchess of Burgundy.

The six years Anne lived at the French court encompassed a lifetime of cultural upheaval for a teenage girl and a revolutionary religious epoch for Europe. For those who prefer their history blocked into memorable segments, the Reformation is often said to have started when the German Augustinian monk Martin Luther in 1517 publicly posted his Ninety-Five Theses condemning the Catholic Church for fund-raising by demanding money for the remission of sins. He regarded such clerical commercialism as blatant misuse of spiritual power for corrupt secular purposes. The Church indulged in the poor taste of putting this practice to rhyme: 'as soon as coin in coffer rings the soul from purgatory springs'. Luther was ordered by the pope to recant his views; he refused, and four years later was excommunicated. To almost everyone's surprise, out of a relatively minor theological squabble swiftly emerged a major international crisis of faith. Standing behind the Ninety-Five Theses was long-existing frustration with the growing materialism of both the theology and behaviour of the Church. As the zeal of the old Church waned and its leadership became increasingly mired in fund-raising and worldly politics, people of tender conscience found themselves dissatisfied with the prescribed formula – a delicate balance between faith in divine grace and good works such as endowing a monastery, giving alms to the poor and hearing mass – whereby the faithful strove to attain paradise. In Germany, Martin Luther in his despair threw inkpots at the devil and sought salvation through the meticulous obedience to monastic discipline – ceaseless payer, vigils and mortification of the flesh. 'If ever,' he confessed, 'a monk got to heaven by monkery it was I.'[18] You could not, he determined, barter your way into heaven.

Had Luther stood alone nothing much would have happened, but it soon became apparent that devout Christians throughout Europe, especially in the universities and courts of kings, were experiencing the same religious anxiety. In England at his college in Cambridge, the scholar Thomas Bilney suffered the same sense of spiritual anguish as Luther in his monastery. He reacted in much the same way: mindless obsession with ritual, 'a scrupulous holiness' that bound him to 'observe the word of Christ after the very letter', and because 'our Lord biddeth us when we will pray [to] enter into our chamber and shut the door', he thought it a 'sin to say his service abroad and always would be sure to have his chamber door shut' when saying his matins. But Thomas Bilney could no more shut the door on doubt than Martin Luther. For both men the fear remained that they did not deserve God's mercy.[19]

Luther and thousands of others found solace in the Bible as the wellspring of hope and resurrection, and it is at this point the religious reformation of the sixteenth century changed from an event into a process; for dependence on the Bible for renewal of personal faith was the altarpiece of Christian humanism, which in its classical form had been captivating the universities of Europe for 100 years before Luther was born. Starting as a passionate admiration for Greek and Roman culture and philosophy with its heavy emphasis on the dignity of the individual, Christian humanism metamorphosed into a belief that faith was a personal contract between a caring and merciful god and the individual, who interpreted god's word as expressed in Scripture for himself without institutional help. Desiderius Erasmus of Rotterdam was the most distinguished Christian humanist of his day and it was no accident that both he and Luther translated the Bible. Erasmus, as a scholar, went back to the original Greek of the New Testament to find the unadulterated words of God and in 1516 published his scholarly rendition of Scriptures. Six years later in 1522 Luther turned the Latin words, understood by few, into the vernacular of German, and he used Erasmus's biblical text to do it. There were no ground rules for Christian humanists, and they varied in both intensity and doctrine from devout orthodox Catholics to secular-minded materialists or spiritually disturbed crypto-Protestants. How exactly to define a Christian humanist has caused Anne's biographers endless difficulties and involves serious semantic debate.

4. Desiderius Erasmus, the leading humanist of his century, friend and admirer of Henry VIII and a profound influence on Anne Boleyn.

A profound truth was emerging; not only could the individual find salvation for himself through the inspiration of the Bible but he did not need good works, clerical ritual or even the mass to open up the gates of heaven. Luther read in the words of St Paul that the 'just shall live by faith', and he rejoiced that he suddenly felt himself 'reborn and to have gone through open doors into paradise. The whole of Scripture took on a new meaning.' Bilney read, 'It is a true saying, and worthy of all men to be embraced, that Christ Jesus came into the world to save sinners,' and he exulted that he had found 'marvellous comfort and quietness insomuch that my bruised bones leaped with joy.'[20] Both men discovered that it was not necessary to warrant salvation. God's grace stood above justice. No amount of striving, no proliferation of good works, could earn a Christian a place in heaven, for God saved even the undeserving. Faith alone could move mountains and save sinners and throw open the gates of heaven. In the meantime, Erasmus, like so many other scholars, sat on the fence, reluctant to allow his scholarship to be degraded by religious polemics. He admitted he had 'laid the egg that Luther hatched' but 'had expected quite another kind of bird' to emerge, one that would unite Christendom in a purified Europe-wide faith, 'an age of gold if ever there was one', not two centuries of theological quarrels and war. And so with alarming speed the Reformation began to break up into splinter groups. During most of Anne Boleyn's stay in Paris, the religious battle stormed in an ever-increasing whirlwind of violence and brutality as Parisian artisans protested and German peasants revolted.

Exactly where or how her religious beliefs emerged is, like almost everything else about Anne, a matter of conjecture. She certainly came from a Christian humanist-inclined family. Sir Thomas, her father, was a patron of and in regular correspondence with Erasmus. Her younger brother George may well have been a more radical reformer than his sister and he certainly was far more articulate for Anne never put pen to paper on the subject of theology. Most of our knowledge of her faith is the result of extrapolation from what she read, which was almost entirely in French. She read the works of Jacques Lefèvre d'Etaples, the scholarly biblical professor at the University of Paris who wrote and thought in the style of Erasmus, refusing to become a Lutheran radical and trying to pump new spiritual blood into the ancient doctrines of the Catholic Church. She certainly knew or knew of Marguerite of Angoulême, the French king's quirky sister who favoured religious reform, associated with the poor and wrote unorthodox verse, the most famous being translated by Anne Boleyn's daughter, Elizabeth, as *A Godly Meditation of the Soul*. There is little doubt that Anne was heavily influenced by Christian humanism and was deeply wedded to reading the Bible in English and French. Whether she was also a crypto-Protestant committed to something recognisable as Protestantism and tried to introduce that creed into England is a matter of considerable dispute, and is better left to chapter 4, when as queen she was in a position to implement her beliefs.

Eventually time and destiny caught up to Anne. She was of marriageable age and she expected to play the role required of all daughters of ambitious gentlemen – marry and enhance the economic and political position of her family. The summons back to England came in 1521 and had to do with her father's quest for the Irish Earldom of Ormonde. Sir Thomas Boleyn's father had married Margaret Butler, the daughter of the Earl of Ormonde. When the earl died without a direct male heir, Sir Thomas as a close friend and important officer of the Tudor monarch was granted the right to display the livery and title of his mother's estates. This, however, conflicted with the Irish claims of Piers Butler, cousin to the old earl and for years acting as the earl's representative in Irish politics and openly styling himself Earl of Ormonde. Butler was immensely useful to Wolsey in keeping the Irish clans loyal and peaceful and his son James was being educated in Wolsey's household in London. The position of young James was open to debate; Wolsey said he was simply a page and student in his home; Piers said that he was in fact a prisoner and hostage to his father's loyalty and pro-English behaviour. The situation reached a crisis when Thomas Howard, now Duke of Norfolk and Thomas Boleyn's father-in-law, was appointed Lord Lieutenant of Ireland. He came up with an excellent paper solution to the disputed earldom: young James Butler and Anne Boleyn should marry. No one would question Piers's claim to the title and a future son would resolve the argument. Wolsey, who was loath to give up James as a hostage for his father's good behaviour, was not enthusiastic about the proposed marriage and was busy with more pressing diplomatic matters on the Continent. He delayed making any decision, and Sir Thomas, caught between angering Wolsey and pushing the duke's solution on the king, ordered his daughter home.

As her father had promised years before, she became one of the queen's maids of honour and was waiting for the king, Cardinal Wolsey and her father to settle the marriage terms between the Boleyn and Butler families. Things were not going well; neither the king nor the Cardinal were enthusiastic, and in all probability Sir Thomas Boleyn was even less pleased – the deal gave the Earldom of Ormonde to Piers Butler for life. Anne was of highly marital age, and if the Butler deal never materialised there were endless other dynastic arrangements to be made. Anne was not a top catch but she was well connected, and all her biographers are agreed she returned to England to get married.

4

The Court of Henry VIII

A number of years ago, it is said, a bishop of the Church of England, after viewing paintings of the six wives of Henry VIII, commented, 'Now I understand why he was so anxious to get rid of them.' By modern standards they were not handsome by far, and one would have thought that a king could have done better. Beauty, however, as we all know, lies more in the eyes of the beholder than in the object observed. From the Gibson girls of the late nineteenth to Marilyn Monroe of the twentieth century beauty resides not in a single feature of the face such as the eyes but in the balance between the eyes, nose and mouth, and the creation of free-flowing hair which is a work of art in its own right. We tend to include a great deal more than just the face; we reckon in the formula for beauty the entire body, and modern clothing reveals as much of the flesh as is socially acceptable. Sixteenth-century standards were quite different. The eyes were the most admired feature of the face, large, lustrous and enticing. The hair is invariably pulled back tightly around the head, framing the face and designed to remind the viewer of a nun's headdress or wimple, the universal symbol of maidenhood. The clothing played little part in enhancing beauty but instead was a status symbol of social position, not of the attraction of the body concealed beneath.

Sometime in 1521, when she was newly arrived in England, Anne was without discernible sexual allure or political experience. She, of course, was a very minor cog in an elaborate machine, and as one of the queen's maids of honour she was expected to wait upon her majesty. Whether she spoke French to her or what they said, we do not know. French was not the queen's natural language but it was the language of diplomacy and Katherine needed practice that was difficult to get at the English court. Anne had little to do during these early years at court except perform as one of the ladies of the court, display her high style, sample the excitement of masculine entertainment, and study the structure of court politics. This last was the final and crucial polish to her education.

Legend has it that Anne had wonderful eyes. Otherwise her looks depend on the prejudices of the observer. Catholics turned her into a monster with goiter or wen on her neck, protruding teeth, sallow skin and a sixth finger revealing her demonic heritage. Friends and future Protestants saw only a delightful young lady with an occasional mole as beauty marks. The Venetian ambassador stood somewhere in between: 'Not one of the handsomest women in the world; she is of middling stature, swarthy complexion, long neck, wide mouth, a bosom not much raised and eyes which are black and beautiful.'[1] There is no definitive portrait of the lady. The one appearing most often in modern biographies with the large letter 'B' hanging from her necklace is of late sixteenth-century origin, and whether it is a true likeness is anybody's guess.

The sexual chemistry that could excite the coldest heart and induce the most freakish actions on the part of men with lustful appetites, even a king, was not slow in appearing. Anne was well aware of her sexual powers and made the most of them. Only days after her death a French poet, Lancelot de Carles, wrote lyrically about her gorgeous eyes, saying that she used them to good 'effect', 'sometimes leaving them at rest, and at others, sending message to carry the secret witness of the heart'.[2] Scarcely a contemporary did not allude to the chemistry that encompassed her, although many attributed it to her French ways and haughty demeanour as she made her presence known in a court mad to copy the height of French fashion in dress, wit, music and courtly love as practised by Mistress Boleyn, just turning twenty.

Unless you believe in the sixteenth-century doctrine of correspondences there is no necessary association between physical looks and character, and it is with her personality that historians have the most trouble. Two alleged characteristics dominate both Anne's reputation and history: extraordinary sex appeal (on which most modern historians agree) and a remarkable talent for manipulating political information to fit her personal or partisan agenda, sometimes called acting as an *agent provocateur*. Sexual attraction and political control melded into a single campaign when Anne learned that the secret to success was control of the king's conversation. For instance, if during an audience an unwelcome subject was brought up, Anne would likely have suggested that Henry end the conversation and attend to the hunt, the masque, or some more pressing issue. If she could not prevent him from listening to opposition advice she could give the audience a favourable spin and interpret it as she desired. If the session was politically friendly to her allies and policies she could allow the conversation to drag on endlessly, but care always had to be taken not to bore the king. Paramours and wives were in an exceptional position to influence the king, and almost everyone was madly envious of Mistress Boleyn.

Very few of the sources go to the extreme of painting her as a cold-blooded opportunist, toying with the king's affection to win herself a crown and marriage with a man she tolerated and was happy to use but did not love. To have done so would have turned a divine-right sovereign into a hapless tool or worse, a fool, not the image of kingship Henry or his subjects could sanction. The politically correct expression was 'not well counselled'. It was always safest to blame a councillor. William Thomas, a staunch company man favourable to the king but no great admirer of the queen, hid behind the customary sixteenth-century conviction that there was a concealed personality lurking behind a pleasant façade: Anne, he reported, was at once 'a wise woman endowed with many good qualities ... but inward she was all another dame than she seemed to be'.[3] Thomas was a firm believer in William Baldwin's advice always to 'look for the cause of everything'. As close as anyone got to portraying Anne as a female version of Shakespeare's Iago, deliberately spreading lies and enjoying dissimulation, was the king's most outspoken critic and cousin, Cardinal Pole, who safe in Rome, branded her the 'cause of all evil'. He wrote Henry after Anne's execution a most undiplomatic letter: 'At your age in life and with all your experience of the world, you were enslaved by your passion for a girl. But she would not give you your will unless you rejected your wife, whose place she longed to take.'[4] At least he did not say she was loveless and yearned only for the babbles and attention bestowed upon a queen.

Anne must have felt reasonably at home in the court of Henry VIII; if you were familiar with one royal household you were knowledgeable with them all. Royal courts tended organisationally to be crowded places filled with 'wolfish cruelty' and 'fox-like subtlety' and were crawling with 'back-friends', secret enemies and cut-throat competitors. Their table clothes were 'black with grease' and 'thou must drink of a common bowl where greasy lips and slimy beard hath been dipped to make some maggot afeared'. The meat was 'lean, tough and old', or it comes to 'board unsavoury and cold', the cheese 'was gnawed with mice or rats or with vile worms'. In sum 'the wretched lazar [leper] with clinking of his bell hath life which doth the courtier's life excels'. The English court, however, was exceptional in one important structural aspect; there were two centres of authority – one in blood and historic theory, the other in ability and fact. And in some ways the de facto sovereign exercised greater power than the legal sovereign. This was partly the result of the king's pleasure; he was still young and vigorous – he had not yet turned thirty – and he was still determined to turn his court into a glittering palace of dance and music, become a war hero and the chivalric pride of England. There was little time for paperwork, which he detested, and he welcomed Thomas Wolsey, who relieved his royal master of most of the burdens of government. In equal part it was also the result of the unprecedented power this cleric and son of an Ipswich butcher and cattle dealer had been able to concentrate about his ample person. He exercised authority that no medieval monarch had even imagined. As Lord Chancellor and cardinal legate, Wolsey united the spiritual and temporal powers of the kingdom. His residences at Hampton Court and York Palace in London housed an entourage fit for a king, 500 courtiers and servants to do his bidding. His cardinal's legatine office brought papal authority directly into England, and both the Archbishop of Canterbury and the humble monk now could be disciplined with a stroke of the pen. As Lord Chancellor, he made the Court of Chancery and the Star Chamber the core of his temporal control, shaking the great barons 'by the ear' and teaching them respect for the king's law. Long before the English king claimed plenary power over his subjects' souls as well as their bodies in the nation state, the cardinal had marked the way.

5. Henry took over Hampton Court Palace from Cardinal Wolsey as being too grand for a fallen and disgraced cardinal. Anne Boleyn had a new queen's suite built but did not survive long enough to enjoy the new luxury.

The keys to Thomas Wolsey's extraordinary success were his unmatched ability to handle details, his understanding of how the royal household worked, and his skill in making the king's will his own. Indeed, the major issue throughout Henry's reign is centred on the question of ultimate responsibility; who actually made policy – king or minister? Today, most historians would agree that policy belonged to the sovereign, its implementation to his minister, whose freedom of action was often so great that at times he shaped and directed policy. This was certainly true of Wolsey, who possessed the added advantage of realising that a successful minister had to control three sources of political authority other than the king's person: first, the privy or secret chamber, whose members waited upon the sovereign's personal needs and were headed by the 'groom of the stool'; second, the great council, directed by the Lord Chancellor, the Lord Privy Seal, the Lord Treasurer and the Principal Secretary; and finally, his astute use of factions to build up a group of people who not only had the king's ear but also were competent and useful members of his government. Factions were not political parties in the modern sense with rights to sponsor and enforce specific policies; those powers belonged to the monarch alone. Instead, they were disparate individuals held together by friendship, blood and opinion who could either bring self- or faction-centred advice to the king or, once policy had been established, get things done. The Wolsey faction was by far the best organised, the cardinal was favoured above all others in his access to the king, and because of his many offices he could reward his loyal following to a degree no one except the monarch could equal.

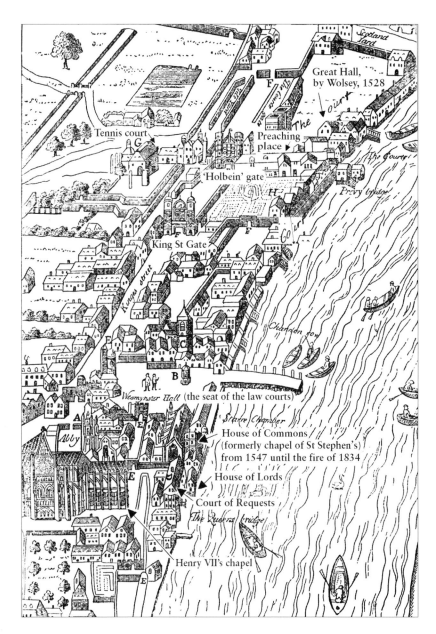

6. A three-dimensional drawing of Westminster and Whitehall Palaces, the centre of Henry VIII's government along the banks of the River Thames just outside of the City of London. What is described as Wolsey's 'Great Hall' was seized by Henry VIII when the cardinal fell from power and became Whitehall Palace.

There were other factions buzzing at court; the oldest was the Plantagenet faction (sometimes called the Aragonese) left over from the fifteenth century. It stemmed from that source of royal fecundity, Edward III and his six sons, and many were distant cousins of Henry Tudor and potential threats to his throne. With royal blood in their veins the Plantagenet faction expanded and contracted over time and included the Neville, Stafford, Pole and Courtenay families, many members of which were intimate with the king and all were close friends and future supporters of Katherine of Aragon. As a political alliance they found themselves more and more in opposition to the king and his domestic and foreign policies. Moreover, their royal heritage made them so dangerous to the House of Tudor that before the end of the reign had executed as many of them as it could manage. Long-term opposition to the crown was extremely dangerous. The safest route was that of the astute cardinal who, according to George Cavendish, his Gentleman Usher, had thrived over the years by practising the principle 'to satisfy the king's mind, knowing right well that it was the very vein and right course to bring him to high promotion'.[5]

Although little is known about Anne's early years at the court, there was one purported sexual relationship between her and Henry Percy, future Earl of Northumberland, which set the stage for Anne's alleged

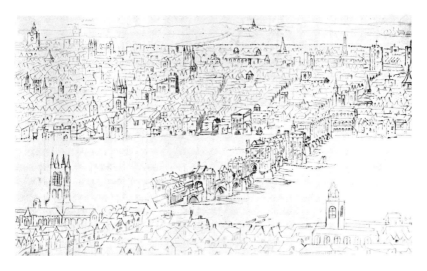

7. London Bridge, where the heads of traitors were displayed on poles. The River Thames was the main commercial thoroughfare linking the east and west sides of the city and was the gateway to all of Henry VIII's many palaces, with Greenwich Palace downstream and Hampton Court upstream.

future hostility to Cardinal Wolsey. Cavendish, a well-placed contemporary writing from memory a generation later, recorded in considerable detail Anne's encounter with the youthful and not very stable Henry Percy. Percy was an emotional character who had considerable trouble coping with the realities of the world in which he lived and the political responsibilities expected of the eldest son of the Earl of Northumberland. During the Pilgrimage of Grace rebellion of 1536, the most serious political upheaval of the reign, he was expected to command the king's forces, but he quietly hid away in Wressle Castle and did nothing while one of his brothers chose martyrdom and the rebel side against the crown. As the early encounter with Anne Boleyn is told by George Cavendish, young Percy was attached to the cardinal's household and on a trip to court fell 'in dalliance among the queen's maidens, being at the last more conversant with Mistress Anne Boleyn than with any other, so that there grew such a secret love between them that at length they were ensured together intending to marry'. Wolsey was not pleased. He and the young man's father had plans, dating many years back, for a Percy–Talbot marriage linking the earldoms of Northumberland and Shrewsbury. Anne's sex appeal was jeopardising an important political arrangement, and in no uncertain terms he marvelled at Percy's 'peevish folly that wouldest tangle and insure thyself with a foolish girl yonder at the court. I mean, Anne Boleyn.' He then reminded him of 'the state that God hath called thee unto in this world, for after the death of thy noble father thou art most like to inherit and possess one of the most worthiest earldoms in this realm'. He then forbid Percy seeing Anne again, and called in his father for a public dressing down. The old earl did not mince his words, branding his son 'a proud, presumptuous, disdainful, and very unthrifty waster', and he threatened to disinherit him. Young Percy, never a pillar of strength to begin with, broke down and accepted his fate with Mary Talbot. Wolsey arranged for an invalidation of any legal marital commitment that

Percy might have made with Anne, and for good measure had the young lady bundled out of court back to her home in Kent.

Like most documents connected with Anne, what appears as a straightforward tale is open to doubt because not only was it written long after the event but its dates are more than a little vague – 1522–4 as a guess – and its author has a clear agenda: he is anxious to display Anne's 'implacable' hatred of Wolsey and date her determination to destroy him politically from the moment Wolsey ruined her chance to marry Henry Percy. She also may have been less than pleased by the suggestion that she was not good enough to wed a Northumberland earl, and, according to Cavendish, she threatened 'if it lay ever in her power, she would work the cardinal as much [i.e. similar] displeasure (as she did indeed after)'.[6]

Far less well documented or politically important was a second sexual partner alleged by later historians determined to create an amorous relationship between Anne and the century's foremost poet, Thomas Wyatt. The account, again undated, that Anne and Thomas Wyatt were bed pals is far more dubious than the possibility that Anne was engaged to Henry Percy; it is the result of Wyatt's often imponderable poetry in the hands of interpreters with hopelessly overheated imaginations. There is not a single line of his verse that can withstand the scepticism of a convinced 'doubting Thomas' to prove that the poet ever had sexual intercourse with Mistress Boleyn. The genesis of the tale is mostly hearsay reported by Thomas Wyatt's grandson George as told to him by two octogenarians, his mother and a venerable attendant of Anne, and supplemented by some highly dubious Spanish documentation.[7] The thought of her marriage to Henry Percy conjures up nothing but disaster; the idea of anything more than a stylised game of courtly love with Wyatt is fanciful myth. Wyatt was certainly a neighbour of the Boleyns in Kent but there is no evidence of a childhood friendship. He met her first at court although there are stories to the contrary. In all probability he was an admirer of the sparkling and much talked-about lady. The only concrete evidence we have that contemporaries, other than Catholic propagandists, believed in some sort of liaison between them is the fact that after Anne's imprisonment in 1536 Wyatt was arrested for a short time, indicating that he was regarded as being of the Boleyn faction, and one of the queen's frequent visitors in her privy chambers. Most of Anne's biographers have been very cautious in recounting the Wyatt–Boleyn relationship.

8. Sir Thomas Wyatt, foremost poet of his century and privy councillor. His sexual relations with Anne Boleyn remain a matter of intense debate.

Most lives follow a fairly rigid routine that gives shape and substance to our existence, but in Anne's case we know nothing about her first four years at court, and the date of the king's interest in the young lady is pure conjecture. As a result the historian is at liberty to allocate dates as he sees fit. Some see Wolsey fronting for the king in his handling of the Percy affair, and his stern efforts to abort the marriage as a way of clearing the field for his sovereign. Others would have Henry both cognisant of Wyatt's alleged passion for Mistress Boleyn and dangerously jealous of the poet. Eric Ives prefers a date after both affairs have run their course and the king is bedded down with Anne's sister Mary Boleyn; he selects the court festivities at Shrovetide in 1526 for the moment when the chivalric and stylised courtly affection of the king turned into carnal love.

Professor Ives's dating gives us a precise moment when the court was enjoying itself and openly thinking of sex; it also allows speculation whether Henry was making invidious comparisons between the sisters. Mary, except for her reputation in bed, was not very exciting; the untested, witty and sparkling Anne may have had far more to offer. Whatever the exact moment, a colossal change was about to take place: the monarch's interest in Anne left her alone both as the sole attraction for the king's fancy and in that no other male would dare express even his courtly love of her. We ought to be able to narrate in detail the growth of this affection because history possesses seventeen love letters addressed to Anne and written by the king himself, despite his well-recorded dislike of setting pen to paper. Except for the crucial information that Henry was head over heels in love, the letters tell us nothing for certain. They are mostly written in French, a few in English; none are dated and they contain almost no historic details from which an order of dating or writing can be derived.

Eric Ives makes much of the love letters, using them to date Henry's offer of marriage and Anne's acceptance. In one of the letters, written while Anne was presumably away from court at Hever Castle and purported to be early in the ordering, Henry comes close to commanding Anne to commit herself: 'If it shall please you to do me the office of a true, loyal mistress and friend and to give yourself up body and soul, to me ... I will take you for my only mistress, rejecting from thought and affection all others save yourself, to serve you only.'[8] Anne's reaction to the royal decree to attend his person and join his bed, which reeked of *droit de seigneur*, is said to have been downright angry. She 'fell down upon her knees, saying I think your majesty … speaketh these words in mirth to prove me, without intent of defiling your princely self … I have already given my maidenhead into my husband's hands' (meaning some future husband).[9] Henry apologised profusely for what was described as 'his great folly'. Most of this is hearsay, but Henry did receive a letter from Anne in which she enclosed a gift, '*une étrenne*', a toy ship with a woman as passenger, displaying a diamond about her neck. In the language of courtly love the boat offered the lady protection and the diamond spoke of the willingness of her heart. The gift according to Ives, was saying yes, the lady would be his future wife. She had, as promised, kept her maidenhood for her husband. At least this was Henry's interpretation, and he wrote back ecstatically that his heart was dedicated to her alone, he wished that his body could be as well, and that he prayed to God every day that 'my prayer will be heard, wishing the time brief, and thinking it but long until we shall see each other again'. Then he signed himself 'that secretary who in heart, body and will is your loyal and most ensured servant'.[10] Whether Anne's yes meant her willingness to become Henry's spouse or simply his full-time mistress is not at all clear although Professor Ives strongly advocates the former.

Unfortunately Anne's letters to the king are not extant and we only have his exuberant reaction to Anne's words to surmise that Henry had proposed and Anne had accepted. He was certainly inordinately pleased about something and it may well have been her acceptance of marriage. If so, marriage changed everything, and it immediately entangled Henry's ardour for a young lady of his court with the king's 'great matter' – he now had to rid himself of Katherine of Aragon, his wife of almost twenty years.

Henry's letters may give us an important date in the king's love life, but they open up a larger and possibly more important problem in his relations with Anne: who was holding out on whom? The letters are always used as firm evidence that Anne was deliberately staying away from court and refusing to become the king's mistress because (and here we arrive at the reader's choice) she believed in the principle of marriage and refused carnal pleasure until properly wed, or she was endeavouring to manipulate the king using his lust to entice him into marriage. Either way, it took Anne six years to get pregnant by the king and finally manoeuvre him into marriage. Exactly what Anne desired is left in studied vagueness.

9. Whitehall Palace down the river from Westminster Palace and the Abbey, drawn by Anthony van Wyngaede. The building was originally the London home of Cardinal Wolsey and known as York House. It was taken over by the king after the cardinal's fall from power and became Anne Boleyn's residence before her actual marriage to Henry, thereby allowing Henry to keep both his Spanish queen and his English fiancé close by.

Two of our biographers have provided opinions concerning the 'hold out' controversy. Eric Ives argues the orthodox view that only Anne was responsible for a six-year engagement and her refusal to marry her sovereign was a matter of principle. There is nothing in the letters to deny this interpretation but there is also no mention that she ever demanded a marriage proposal as the key to her virginity.[11] In contrast, G. W. Bernard maintains that Henry, realising that taking Anne as his mistress would tarnish the purity of his conscience, and lessen his chances of persuading the pope to grant him an annulment, urged Anne to wait until he could arrange a legal marriage.[12] Their understandable desire to live under the same roof in close proximity to one another carried with it the risk of pregnancy that the king wished to minimise by stern self-denial. The king had already enjoyed kissing Anne's 'pretty dukkys', and he needed all the self-control he could muster. As Jean du Bellay, the French ambassador, rather caustically summed up the situation, 'If the belly grows, all will be spoilt.'[13] Since we do not have Anne's responses to the king's letters either verbal or epistolary, what she wanted is sheer surmise. She may have, as Ives attests, planned all along to marry the king, or as Bernard prefers, have sought protection from what happened to her sister, who had been the king's mistress for less than a year and had been quickly discarded and forgotten. Presumably Anne was angling for a long-term commitment from the king before becoming his mistress. Who was holding back and urging restraint? The love letters leave the verdict open. At times the argument seem to be more like a droll wrangle, with Lewis Carroll's Humpty Dumpty pontificating that 'when I use "a word" it means just what I choose it to mean – neither more nor less' than a scholarly debate. Paint a picture of an intelligent sixteenth-century girl who discovers that her sovereign is madly in love with her but can't forget what happened to her sister, and Anne Boleyn's decision to hold out for marriage makes perfectly good sense. Conversely, portray a king obsessed by a highly sensitive conscience who feels obliged to chase after the pope for six years because only a papal dispensation will relieve him of sin and guarantee him future legitimate children, and Henry's actions become even more understandable than Anne's.

5

The King's Great Matter

Acknowledging for the moment that Eric Ives's date of the summer of 1527 was the moment when Henry proposed marriage and Anne accepted, it seems fitting to ask a series of difficult questions about the newly engaged couple: what kind of people were they; except for sexual chemistry, did they have anything in common; and did Henry's decision at the age of thirty-five to ride himself of a forty-year-old frumpy wife have anything to do with his falling madly in love with the vivacious Anne Boleyn? Taking the last query first, Professor Eric Ives strongly argues that Henry's decision to divorce his wife came at least a year before he proposed to Anne; it probably corresponded with his decision in 1524 to quit sleeping with his queen, who had not conceived in seven years. Their marriage, by royal standards, had been reasonably successful until Katherine grew too old to perform her cardinal function of producing heirs to the throne. She had had multiple miscarriages and stillbirths but only one living offspring, Princess Mary. Henry had known Katherine ever since she arrived in England in 1502 to marry his older brother Prince Arthur. Katherine's marriage lasted only four months, and when Arthur died, Henry, aged eleven, found himself heir apparent and engaged to his widowed sister-in-law. After almost seven years of on again, off again engagement to satisfy the needs of his father's erratic dynastic polices, he elected after his father's death in 1509 to do the gentlemanly thing and marry a damsel who had been in great distress for the past seven years.

Rumours of a divorce had been current as early as 1522 when Henry's daughter Mary was being discussed as a possible bride for the French king. Ives's purpose is to protect the validity of the king's conscience, which he insists was the sole explanation for claiming that the king's marriage to Katherine of Aragon was invalid.[1] She had been married to his deceased brother Arthur and not even a papal dispensation could set aside the biblical prohibition stated in Leviticus 20:21: 'If a man shall take his brother's wife it is an unclean thing ... he shall be without children.' By placing the decision to have the marriage annulled well before his passion for Anne had appeared, both the king and his biographer escape the charge that conscience was being made a cover-up for lust. Nothing could be allowed to weaken the strength and intensity of the king's conscience, which is seen as the driving force behind the six-year engagement to Anne Boleyn.

Unfortunately the first indisputable date tying Anne to the king's conscience is August of 1527 when Henry applied to and received from Rome a papal dispensation allowing him to marry the sister of someone with whom he had had illicit sex, 'even one with whom he himself had had intercourse already'.[2] What Henry's purpose was in asking for this dispensation is unclear. It sounds like an invitation, presumably to Anne Boleyn, to hop into (or back into) his bed, and we can well imagine Cardinal Wolsey admonishing his master that if she did, his persistent assertion that he was requesting an annulment of his marriage solely for reasons of conscience would be immediately laughed out of court. Although we do not know what Anne's response was to the papal bull hypothetically permitting the king to marry the sister of his mistress, Henry seemed fully satisfied. He obviously did not anticipate any delay on the pope's part in granting him an annulment; he hadn't as yet even asked for her hand in marriage. In all likelihood the 1527 dispensation was part of the king's campaign to lure Anne into his bed. The only conscience that might have been pricked by copulating with Henry was Mary Boleyn's sister, Anne's. If this is correct, Anne appears as a far more traditional Catholic than usually presented. In the end it was a wise precautionary move for five year later Anne was still unmarried but pregnant by the king. The fact still remains, however, that the date August 1527 is close enough to when the king's conscience was pierced to soil his motives, and the legend, in Shakespeare's phraseology, that the king's conscience 'crept too near another lady' of the court has thrived ever since despite Eric Ives's efforts to suppress it.

That Henry's conscience might have been sullied by his passion for Anne did not trouble him in the least for, as he informed his nephew-in-law, Emperor Charles V, he could not 'quiet or appease his conscience remaining longer with the queen whom, for her nobleness of blood and other virtues, he had loved entirely as his wife, until he saw in Scripture that God had forbidden their union'.[3] For Henry the issue was both simple and far reaching: 'All such issue males as I have received of the queen died immediately after they were born: so that I fear the punishment of God in that behalf.'[4] He believed as a man and as a divine-right monarch that not only was he on speaking terms with his deity but also that God could be coaxed by prayer and ritual into granting the desires and needs of man, especially when that man was a high priest and expert on all things theological and ecclesiastical.

It is understandable that in a volume on Anne Boleyn the husband does not receive top billing but biologically he deserves half-credit, and his role as sovereign requires far more attention than a normal spouse might deserve. None of the four authors, not even Alison Weir, who covers only the last three and a half months of the story, give Henry the space his kingship requires or go into the nature of his religious beliefs and the structure of his thinking. From childhood on Henry had been deeply inculcated in the religious orthodoxy of his century, and according to Sebastian Giustinian, the Venetian ambassador, he was 'very religious; heard three masses daily when he hunted, and sometimes five on other days' besides attending vespers and complines.[5] There was a rumour that before his elder brother Arthur died Henry was being educated to become an archbishop, and long before 1521 when it appeared in print, the king was labouring on his *Assertio Septem Sacramentorum*, his scholarly and highly popular attack against Martin Luther's heresy. The immaculate regulation of divine ritual was the very least a semi-divine and learned sovereign could do to display his faith in a deity who had created him and endowed him with the responsibilities of kingly office. His authority stemmed from 'God, being in the room that I am in'.[6] Many times over Henry Tudor reiterated the creed of duty: the higher the human rank the greater the divine responsibility. As Thomas Aquinas maintained, kings carried a greater duty than other men and could expect 'a high degree of heavenly happiness'.[7] When his archbishop wrote that man is saved by his faith in Christ's passion and death, he insisted on adding the phrase 'I doing my duty'. Christians might be, he confessed, the inheritors of God's kingdom but only so long as they 'preserve in His precepts and laws'. To the suggestion that the adversities that plague humanity should be attributed to God's will, he sternly added that misfortunes were the result of man's 'own desert'.[8] Henry was not merely a religious nitpicker, he always demanded concrete evidence of faith in terms of obedience to man's law, and early in his theological development in his learned attack on Martin Luther he voiced a creed in which he never wavered: there is far greater need 'to contemplate the severe and inflexible justice of God' than the uncertainty of his mercy.[9] Faith alone was far too uncertain and far too dangerously individualistic.

It never occurred to him that his own brand of faith in the correctness of his reading of Leviticus and his insistence that God worked in terms of quid pro quo – obey my laws and be rewarded – was equally individualistic and intense.

Henry's satisfaction with his relationship with his deity was stated many times over but never more poignantly than when he informed the Venetian ambassador that he could not 'see that there is any faith in the world, save in me, and therefore God Almighty, who knows this, prospers my affairs'.[10] Many years later in his editing of the *Bishops' Book* he stated the same confidence except in reverse. Henry made divine protection conditional upon good behaviour: God's protection was 'void' if 'I continued in sin'.[11] It followed then that if the deity turned his back upon a man and beset him with earthly and dynastic troubles, somehow, somewhere that man had sinned. There could be no greater evidence of divine displeasure than a series of miscarriages and stillbirths and the jeopardising of Henry's entire purpose on earth – the survival and continuation of his masculine sperm to secure an undisputed succession. The sovereign of conscience, who was a confirmed ritualist and a divine-right monarch who of necessity had ruled out all doubt and could do no wrong, can be a far more ruthless suitor than a lover blinded by an excess of testosterone.

His conscience was impervious to doubt and the ridicule of Christendom. That his wife Katherine had sworn that she had come to Henry's bed a virgin, that her marriage to Arthur had been in name only, and that he had died before they had had sexual intercourse were all lies. Her words had to be untrue for they were contrary to his greater knowledge of God's will. The dispensation of the pope was equally worthless for the actions of a mere man could not negate the evidence of divine wrath displayed in the death of all of his children except Princess Mary. Henry knew that he had sinned in marrying Arthur's wife, and nothing would ever pardon that sin except the legal annulment of the marriage and the chance to start afresh with a new wife. Evil and sin were real and ever-present obstacles to the well-adjusted man, but for the king they invariably resided outside of him and could be mitigated by attending to the proper ritual. Religion was a bargain between man and God in which both elements knew the rules and penalties. In his own life he expected no less. He had fought mightily to defend the Church against the Lutheran heresy, and he now expected a proper return on his labours. He wrote Clement VII that 'the favour' of an annulment, which 'for the first time we ask of your holiness ... cannot justly be denied to our piety and our efforts and endeavours for the Catholic cause'.[12]

The moment that Henry's steel-encased conscience demolished his instinctive respect for papal authority, and he finally took to heart Sir Thomas More's warning that the Holy Father was a political figure against whom a secular prince might someday find himself at odds, his tendency, as Eustace Chapuys remarked, was to 'go the whole length'. If the Bishop of Rome was a mere politician then might not all bishops be political creatures using their claim to divine status above all other ranks as a cloak for nefarious and worldly actions? Anti-clericalism and the royal conscience conjoined to forge a sovereign profoundly suspicious of all priestly authority, especially if it in any way competed with royal authority. When his prelates in an early draft of the *Bishops' Book* in 1537 suggested that 'it belongeth unto the jurisdiction of priests and bishops' to regulate and decide on the ceremonial life of the Church, Henry inserted a warning that clerical authority was not to be regarded as divine authority and added the secular safeguard that priestly power must be 'overseen and approved by the King's Highness and his Council'; only then were subjects 'bound to obey'. Henry clearly viewed his clergy as civil servants of a crown imbued with divine spirit.

The king's firm opposition to clerical marriages was grounded on the same fear that the clergy would upset the balance of a properly run commonwealth. He worried lest 'priests would so increase in number by affinity and descent' that they would tyrannise all temporal authority and make themselves hereditary. The doctrine of human prudence in managing both Church and state was high on the king's agenda. Lutheranism and Protestantism, he maintained, robs princes of all power and authority; for what shall a king do 'if he cannot appoint any law but like a ship without a rudder suffer his people to float from land'? Even the Lord's Prayer required caution, particularly the suggestion that 'our daily bread' might be the fruits of God's grace and not of man's labour. The same circumspection applied to Christian charity.

'One thing herein is to be noted'; there were many people who would rather live 'by craft of begging slothfully than either work or labour for their living'. Henry to his dying day never varied from the doctrine of good works, man's free will to take full responsibility for his actions, and a subject's absolute duty to obey the law as prescribed by the monarch.

In all likelihood the king's redoubtable if troubled conscience did not emerged fully armed with verses of Leviticus from Henry's fertile mind, although Ives treats it as it were an epiphany; like Topsy, it simply grew in the years before 1526 when there was more than enough evidence of divine displeasure. In 1524 the king entered a joust with the Duke of Suffolk with the visor of his helmet wide open; the duke's spear missed his unprotected face by half an inch. The following year Henry came even closer to death and in a far more humiliating fashion. He had been out hawking, was chasing an injured bird through a swampy area, tried to jump a ditch, broke his jumping pole and fell head first into the water, his head stuck in the mud. His attendants reached him just in time to save him from being smothered to death. In 1528 his chronic headaches began and shortly thereafter he experienced the first pains of gout. Everything seemed to remind the king that God had turned his face against him, and as a man and a Christian he had but one recourse – to reassert his conscience which was, he said, right 'not because so many said it', but because he as a man and as a king 'knoweth the matter was right'.[13] Though 'the law of everyman's conscience,' he asserted, 'be but a private court, yet it is the highest and supreme court for judgement or justice.'[14] For all of the depth of the ocean that divided Henry Tudor and Martin Luther, the water was strikingly the same – both were men of overactive conscience, except Luther called it justification by faith alone.

Henry's religious growth can be recorded and documented; Anne's, alas, cannot. However, enough is known to say with some certainty that she was an orthodox Catholic with Christian humanistic leanings who was close enough to Henry's own brand of orthodoxy to have asked William Kingston, when she was imprisoned in the Tower, 'Shall I be in heaven for I have done many good deeds in my day?'[15] Her husband would have approved of those words – he believed firmly in deeds winning a place in paradise. Except for their mutual abhorrence of the pope and the king's anti-clericalism both were confirmed if occasionally unpredictable Catholics. Anne may well have been overly biblical in her religious tastes but the king always enjoyed a sound ecclesiastical debate. Add to this they both were musical, spoke French and could turn the dullest subject into interesting words and ideas, and it is safe to say they had as much in common as any freshly engaged couple.

Henry anticipated no trouble over his annulment. The pope was already in his debt, and as late as 1529, when he wrote Emperor Charles for support, he was still asking his imperial nephew whether he would 'willfully destroy' Henry's soul by refusing his help in the dissolution of such an unlawful union. No Christian could possibly vote against him. Henry was always a confirmed optimist – being on speaking terms with your deity demands a highly sanguine personality – but, though the king would not admit it, the international situation was not propitious for a favourable solution to the Henry's great matter.

In 1525, Emperor Charles of the Holy Roman Empire and Francis Valois of France did final battle at Pavia for the mastery of Italy. The French were badly defeated and the Most Christian King of France was taken prisoner. Charles was conqueror of Italy and Leviathan of Europe. Two years later, just as Henry's courtship with Anne Boleyn was moving towards a marriage proposal, imperial troops sent to Rome mutinied for lack of pay and sacked the city. The pope took refuge in the papal Castel Sant'Angelo and it was obvious to all, except possibly the King of England, that his holiness was no longer a free agent but an imperial flunky, doing the emperor's bidding. He was, he confessed, ready 'to live and die an imperialist'. Charles, in effect speaking for the pope, made it clear he would protect his aunt's marriage rights. Back in England the situation was becoming critical. Katherine was adamant that her marriage was legal and her daughter Mary the undisputed heir; Henry took steps to advertise the presence of his ten-year-old illegitimate son, Henry Fitzroy, and had him promoted to the rank of Duke of Richmond, a honour that gave him precedence at court over any other title, badly upsetting the queen, and in 1529 Henry began to hint broadly to the pope of the possible financial and legal consequences of any failure to grant him an annulment from his fat, sterile forty-four-year-old wife.

The pope, desperate to find a compromise satisfactory to two stubborn men – king and emperor – turned to a series of rather tawdry solutions. Clement VII would grant a dispensation sanctioning incest and marry off the illegitimate Duke of Richmond to his half-sister Princess Mary, who in her father's eyes was equally illegitimate. He urged Henry to take Anne as his mistress and promised to legitimise their children born out of wedlock. He discretely suggested that Katherine retire into a nunnery, thereby allowing him to permit the remarriage of her husband. He even toyed with the notion of bigamy, permitting Henry two wives at the same time. All these questionable ideas fell foul of both Henry's tender conscience and greatest need – a legitimate male heir. Only the pope could salve the first or supply the second. The papacy had started the whole thing by violating divine law laid down in Leviticus and it was up to the pope to make amends and rid Henry of the taint of sin by dissolving the marriage and accepting God's law. Only then would a future heir to the throne be legitimate and beyond dispute.

Just exactly how literal and intense the king's conscience was is revealed by the remarkable silence of all sixteenth-century documents about one possible but never-mentioned answer to the king's marital problems – the quiet murder of the queen.[16] Murder was no anathema to the century, and

Katherine's death by poison was talked about after Anne became queen. Henry's daughter Elizabeth suggested discreet assassination as her preferred way of disposing of her dynastic dilemma – Mary, Queen of Scots. Henry himself was not averse to sanctioning the death of Cardinal David Betoun, the leader of the pro-French party in Scotland and a dangerous thorn in Henry's diplomacy, but he wisely never put it in writing. That political murder never even seems to have been discussed can only be explained in terms of the king's conscience and insistence at least until 1532 on legitimacy, both of his offspring's birth and his queen's death. By 1529 he was starting to give up asking the pope to grant him an annulment, and was seriously thinking about accepting his French brother sovereign's advice to go it alone. The pope had accepted Katherine's appeal to Rome, and Henry was faced with the real possibility that he might be called to Rome to defend his case. Little wonder he was seriously thinking of following Francis I's advice to divorce Katherine, marry Anne and wait and see what Emperor Charles and the pope would do, which, Francis predicted, would be very little except for several years of threatening talk.

The year 1529 was for the king's great matter a momentous twelve months; Henry began to slide into outright defiance of the papacy; the international treaty of Cambrai was signed between the Habsburg Empire and France, much to England's disadvantage; and Cardinal Wolsey fell from power. Thomas Wolsey had been at the centre of English politics and diplomacy for almost twenty years. In September he was deprived of his office of Lord Chancellor and a month later was accused of high treason for having violated, when he accepted his legatine powers from the papacy, the fourteenth-century statute of praemunire that forbade Roman authority being enforced in England. Who orchestrated his downfall is a matter of historical controversy stemming from the existence of contradictory documentation. Condemning Anne Boleyn and portraying her as the cardinal's evil nemesis is George Cavendish's message in his *Life and Death of Cardinal Wolsey*. Cavendish's biography is a reasonably even-handed work except for his intense dislike of Anne, whose own hatred for Wolsey is presented as going back to when Wolsey blocked her marriage to Henry Percy. Ives quotes Cavendish with great favour:

> The great lords of the council, bearing secret grudge against the cardinal because they could not rule in the commonweal as they would ... caught an occasion to invent a means to bring him out of the king's high favour ... They knew right well that it was very difficult for them to do anything directly themselves, wherefore they perceiving the great affection that the king bare lovingly unto Mistress Anne Boleyn, fantasying in their heads that she should be for them a sufficient and apt instrument to bring their malicious purpose to pass ... And she having a very good wit, and also an inward desire to be revenged of the cardinal was agreeable to their requests ...

On these grounds, Ives maintains, Anne 'entered politics' and began establishing a Boleyn faction consisting of her father and brother in league with the Dukes of Norfolk and Suffolk.[17] They used two serious setbacks to the king's efforts to get a quick and easy annulment to his marriage as their weapons to poison Henry's mind against Wolsey. Katherine was successful in appealing her defence of her marriage to the king to Rome, and Cardinal Lorenzo Campeggio, the papal official in charge of the trial along with Wolsey, had to postpone any final decision. Equally disastrous was the rapprochement at Cambrai between the emperor and Francis I, in which France turned Italy over to Charles, thereby transforming the pope into a Spanish chaplain.

Cardinal Wolsey was responsible for neither of these events but it became increasingly clear that he preferred, if his king were to divorce and remarry, that he wed a foreign princess and not marry Mistress Boleyn.

Except for the cardinal's second thoughts about Anne Boleyn's marital worth, G. W. Bernard will have none of this. He dismisses Cavendish as hopelessly biased and the Norfolk–Boleyn alliance, if it existed at all, as the work of the father, not of the future queen. He bases his interpretation not on the Cavendish biography of Wolsey but on the *Letters and Papers of Henry VIII* in which are recorded the correspondence between Anne and Wolsey. They express both warmth and friendship for one another and far more than professional courtesy on the part of two people working for the same master. Anne made their relationship manifest when she wrote,

> In my most humblest wise that my poor heart can think I do thank you for your kind letter and for your rich and goodly present for which I shall never be able to deserve without your great help of the which I have hitherto had so great plenty that all the days of my life I am most bound ... to love and preserve your grace of the which I beseech you never to doubt that ever I shall vary from this thought as long as [breath] is in my body.[18]

Her run-on sentence is more than a little convoluted but if these words reveal deliberate dissimulation and duplicity as some historians have claimed, then they also disclose surprising mastery of disguise and cunning on the part of both Anne and Wolsey.

In Bernard's estimation, Anne bore Wolsey no ill will; she gained nothing from his fall from grace; and her position was that of a typical sixteenth-century woman who did little other than wait at home. He has no explanation why Cavendish picked Anne as his femme fatale, although he might have pointed out that the sixteenth century invariably, when looking for evil, insisted that the personality and social position should fit the crime. To have arranged the fall of such a successful and powerful man as Wolsey would take a future queen to do the job. For Bernard, Henry was the dominant force in the cardinal's disgrace, and the professor develops the quite plausible thesis that Thomas Wolsey's fall was far more than an English affair; it was a warning to the pope that if he did not give the king his annulment a marital squabble might lead to a constitutional break with Rome. Striking at a cardinal and a papal legate was a useful reminder that Henry could also strike at Rome and renounce the authority of a pope. The king had also become aware that his cardinal might be cool on the Boleyn marriage and feel that she was not worth the trouble she was causing. Any suggestion that Wolsey was not a 100 per cent supporter of Anne was fatal because, as the imperial ambassador put it, 'this king is so blind with passion that there is nothing he will not do or promise to attain his object', not even countenancing the death of his chief minister.[19]

10. Wood carving in Canterbury Cathedral depicting Katherine of Aragon flanked by Cardinals Wolsey (left) and Campeggio (right). The facial expressions reveal the failure of the Blackfriars divorce trial to achieve its purpose in resolving the king's great matter: Wolsey realises the fatal consequence to his career, Katherine is in tears, and Campeggio is playing a secret game of duplicity.

Henry Tudor may have been blinded by sexual passion but the evidence was piling up that God continued to turn his face away from him in an inescapable manner. The legatine court set up at Blackfriars by Cardinals Wolsey and Campeggio in May 1529 with great hope that it would annul his marriage to Katherine and liberate him to marry Anne had turned into a fiasco, with the queen appealing her case to Rome and Campeggio doing nothing to stop it. On top of that, Francis of France and Emperor Charles had made peace at the international conference at Cambrai on 3 August, leaving Italy and the pope to be dictated to by Charles. With her nephew in control, any finding of a papal court would inevitably be against the king. Professor Ives recognises Henry's desperation but with almost no introduction insists, 'he was discovering that he was less than the king God had made him. The drive to marry Anne was not only to satisfy emotion and desire; it became a campaign to vindicate his kingship.'[20] As evidence Ives harkens back to the Hunne case in 1515 when the Church tried to hide behind benefit of clergy, the principle that maintained that it was contrary to the historic law of God to try a cleric in a royal court and a violation of the ancient liberties of the ecclesia as well as a denial of a papal decree protecting priests from all secular authority. The case involved the death in jail of an accused heretic. The Church dismissed the death as the suicide of a deranged criminal; the secular coroner's court, reflecting public anti-clericalism, accused the jailer, the bishop's chancellor, of murder, and the Bishop of London claimed benefit of clergy for his chancellor. Public outcry demanded a public investigation into the Church's right to benefit of clergy with the king presiding. Henry was far more concerned about the clash between Church and state authorities than any injustice done to Hunne. He in no way denied the Church's rights and liberties but came down heavily on the side of royal jurisdiction taking precedent over ecclesiastical. 'Kings of England,' he pronounced, 'have never had any superior but God alone.' He made it clear he was speaking historically and upholding what his ancestors had believed 'in time past'.[21] Unfortunately there is no evidence on the workings of the king's mind in 1529 except on how to stop the pope from ruling in favour of his wife.

Fortunately there were individuals throughout the kingdom giving considerable thought to the question of ultimate authority. Towards the end of 1528 a 'monster petition' signed by the elite of the country was begun begging his holiness to grant the king his divorce on the grounds of national interest. The petition was ready by June 1530, and embedded in the wording was the pregnant threat that should the pope refuse the king's request England would not be 'wholly desperate' because 'it is possible to find relief some other way'.[22] Clement VII was warned many times over that Henry's matrimonial problems might explode into open rebellion against Rome. The possibility that the king might remarry without papal approval, however, was unattractive for two reasons; first and most important it left any child born to such a marriage illegitimate, and second, opposition might be so great as to make the marriage politically impossible. What the king needed was a new and unimpeachable authority to authorise the annulment.

Months earlier, anxious to probe every scholarly path, Henry had authorised a group of clerics and university scholars to study scriptures and patristic writings to discover whether there was historic evidence to prove that the papacy held no supreme authority in matters spiritual. Their conclusion, *Collectanea satis copiosa*, claimed two important findings: first, each province of the early Christian Church had its own laws and jurisdiction with no interference from the pope, and therefore the correct organisation to settle the king's matrimonial problem was the Church of England. And second, that kings stood higher in divine authority than popes. A monarch in his domain was absolutely supreme, answerable to God alone. Here in all probability was the kernel in the king's mind that eventually blossomed into both a new definition of kingship and statehood.

At the same time the king met Thomas Cranmer. In October 1529 the soft-spoken, overly timid forty-three-year-old Cambridge don was ordered to an interview with his sovereign. Cranmer would play a vital role in the English Reformation saga and emerge as one of the most endearing if reluctant of the Protestant martyrs. He was among Anne's few close friends, future godfather to her daughter, but not always an outspoken ally. As always his king came first. During their conference Henry learned of and was impressed by the professor's argument that he did not need papal blessings to achieve a annulment, and that the theological faculties in the universities throughout Europe had the right to pass judgement on such cases. Four months later Cranmer, along with Thomas Boleyn, was on his way to test this theory with only partial success. The new aggressive and rebellious policies of the king reach climax toward the beginning of 1531 when the king determined to use Cardinal Wolsey's treason in violating the ancient statute of praemunire as a way of extracting money from the Church of England as a whole. He threatened to extend Wolsey's crime to the entire Church. Convocation, the ecclesiastical equivalent of parliament, took the hint and offered £100,000 in return for a royal pardon for the possible offence. What caused trouble was not so much the monies involved as the wording of the grant. Henry demanded that his pardon be conditional on Convocation recognising him as 'sole protector and supreme head of the English Church and clergy'. Eventually, Ives thinks at Thomas Cromwell's suggestion, Henry's headship was qualified by the addition of the phrase 'so far as the law of Christ allows'. It was clear to almost everybody that Henry had one definition of the meaning of the 'law of Christ' and the Church another; the clergy thought it negated any idea of the headship; the king, as supreme head, knew he spoke directly for God.[23]

Since no one wanted to debate the issue, the rephrased version of the king's authority over his ecclesia passed Convocation to be argued at a later time. What, however, has not been accepted without debate is Anne Boleyn's involvement in the course of the English Reformation and her influence over the king. Professor Ives portrays Anne as the driving force behind the king's great matter. Henry is scarcely mentioned, and all radicalism is attributed to the Boleyn faction, especially Anne, her father and brother. She goaded her lover into more and more radical words against the pope; she was instrumental in insisting the king meet Thomas Cranmer; and she made 'demonstrations of joy as if she had actually gained paradise' when Convocation knuckled under, paid up and accepted Henry as the qualified Supreme Head of the Church.[24] When he was not 'moving in the direction she wanted' she would nag him to be firmer and brought tears to his eyes with her complaints that he no longer loved her. On St Andrew's Day after supper, with the king and Katherine both present, the royal couple had had a verbal row. Katherine taxed her husband for having neglected her, Henry countered by calling the pope a heretic. Katherine laughed at the thought and Henry walked out in a huff. Anne, according to Eustace Chapuys, took full advantage of the situation:

Did I not tell you that whenever you dispute with the queen she was sure to have the upper hand? I see that some fine morning you will succumb to her reasoning and that you will cast me off. I have been waiting long and might in the meanwhile have contracted some advantageous marriage, out of which I might have had issue, which is the greatest consolation in his world. But, alas! Farewell to mine time and youth spent to no purpose at all.[25]

Since Chapuys detested Anne Boleyn, the twenty-first century may very well accept these almost too perfect words as a true saying and concede that there was a conniving and self-serving element to her character.

Whatever the final analysis on Anne's personality, there is wide disagreement as to her responsibility for the Reformation. Eric Ives gives her full credit as the driving force behind almost every event and makes her the agent through which Henry received all his ideas. Conversely, G. W. Bernard dismisses her as the beloved plaything of a strong-minded king developing his own Reformation policy to achieve his matrimonial ends.[26] Their most flamboyant points of disagreement involve the part Anne played in shaping Henry's mind by introducing him to Simon Fish's *The Supplication of Beggars* and William Tyndale's *Obedience of a Christian Man and How Christian Rulers Ought to Govern*. Both stories owe much to John Foxe's *Acts and Monuments*. There is little doubt that the king knew of, even read, Tyndale's *Obedience of a Christian*

Man but whether he did so at Anne's bidding is a matter of opinion. As the account goes Tyndale, in exile in Europe and branded by the English authorities as a heretic for having translated the Bible into English, wrote the *Obedience* in 1526 and had multiple copies smuggled into England. Anne acquired one, marked passages to show the king, but first lent it to her gentlewoman who had it yanked out of her hands by her suitor and future husband. This young man, anxious to read the forbidden material, got caught doing so by the Dean of the Chapel Royal. On hearing this, to protect both herself and her gentlewoman, Anne went to Henry who not only listened to the story and ordered the book returned to its original owner but also read Anne's marked lines, commenting that 'this book is for me and all kings to read'. Tyndale preached strong but appealing music to the king's ears. 'All men without exception are under the temporal sword, whatsoever names they give themselves.' In other words, the belief that the clergy possessed special powers was contrary to divine truth; no cleric from the pope on down to the parish priest stood outside the king's law. 'One king, one law' was God's decree for 'every realm'. Henry did not have to wait on a cleric in Rome to achieve his annulment. He had sufficient authority in himself. Henry was so delighted by what he read he tried to hire Tyndale to write propaganda for the king's great matter.

Simon Fish was less theoretical but more passionate and entertaining. He was a London lawyer who had written a biting satire against Cardinal Wolsey. He fled to Europe to escape the cardinal's long arm and wrote the *Supplication of Beggars*, a highly anti-clerical plea to Henry to free his Church from rapacious bishops 'munching in their mangers' and tyrannical prelates 'loitering in their lordships'. According to Foxe, Fish's wife sent Anne Boleyn a copy, and after discussing the matter with her brother she gave her copy to the king who read the work, liked it and ordered Fish back to England to receive a pardon. Bernard is doubtful about both tales but does not deny that Henry may have read both works. What he strongly opposes is the hypothesis that Anne's involvement was anything more than an accident. She did not deliberately bring Tyndale and Fish to the king's attention, and she was not the driving force in the Reformation, let alone helping 'conceptualise' Henry's 'instinctive feelings about kingship'.[27]

Most scholars would agree that the turning point in the king's great matter was January 1531 when parliament finally met. It had been originally called to enact attainder legislation against Wolsey for his violation of the statute of praemunire but the cardinal's death had made this unnecessary. Since no one could think of a proper use of parliament, its session had been continuously postponed. With Wolsey's disgrace the management of the king's government was taken over by the Duke of Norfolk, who has had few friendly chroniclers and some would say that he was nothing more than a figurehead for Anne Boleyn and her Boleyn faction. The duke, however, may not be easily applauded but he had a remarkable gift for political survival. The clergy had been brought to heel and had acknowledged Henry as supreme head but with the disturbing proviso 'only so far as the law of Christ allows'. The king was putting increasing pressure on the pope but was still determined to discover some method to guarantee that all future children would be legitimate and not engender civil war over a disputed succession.

11. Thomas Howard, 3rd Duke of Norfolk, Lord Treasurer, premier peer of the kingdom and uncle to two of Henry VIII's wives – Anne Boleyn and Catherine Howard. The duke has had a bad press over the centuries but possessed the gift of political survival.

The problem was what to do now. Who suggested parliament as an authority that could grant the king a legal divorce is speculative. Exactly how Thomas Cromwell and the septuagenarian Christopher St German, author of *Doctor and Student*, a legal treatise urging parliamentary law as superior to ecclesiastical law, came to the king's attention is equally uncertain. St German laid down the concept of crown or king in parliament as being the highest authority in the land. A 'new found article of faith' was being voiced, asserting that a statute made by the authority of the entire realm could not be thought to 'recite a thing against the truth'.[28] Armed with a new authority and Thomas Cromwell's parliamentary skills in implementing German's theories, the pace of the king's great matter began to speed up. Cromwell moved ahead on two fronts. Parliament passed with great hesitancy the first Statute of Annates, giving Henry the right to abolish the traditional payment to the pope of the first year's income from all newly installed bishops and high ecclesiastical officers, and to redirect the funds to the royal exchequer. The purpose was to strike at the papacy at its most vulnerable aspect – its insatiable need for money. Far more revolutionary was the Statute in Restraint of Appeals, which was a blazon signal that the king had decided to go it alone and get his annulment without the pope. By a stroke of the legislative pen in April 1533 parliament reluctantly decreed that all spiritual cases 'shall be from henceforth ... definitely adjudged and determined within the king's jurisdiction and authority' and 'not elsewhere'.²⁹ The last piece fell into place when Archbishop William Warham, who had become increasingly opposed to the king's great matter and particularly its denial of supreme papal authority, died in August of 1532, and Henry's man, Thomas Cranmer, was installed in March according to the ancient and traditional rites as the highest ecclesiastic in the land. The only thing left to be done now was to marry Mistress Anne Boleyn; that occurred on 25 January 1533 (we think).

The order of events during the autumn, winter and spring of 1532–3 are reasonably well attested except for one vital uncertainty; when did Henry and Anne start to cohabit together and who was the initiator? The only fixed date is to work back nine months from the birth of Elizabeth on 7 September 1533; that puts us in early December 1532 as the biological moment when the two made love. Two questions immediately jump to mind; was this the first time they had had met in bed, and if so what persuaded them to have sex? The traditional answer and the one held by Professor Ives is that Anne was a virgin in December 1532. She had held out against the king's passionate desires for six years, and either grew desperate and decided that only physical contact would assure marriage, or she felt that all signs – Warham's death, the forth coming passage of the Statute of Repeals, Cranmer's elevation as archbishop – indicated that Henry was really getting ready to marry her in defiance of the Catholic Church. Ives gives as his crucial evidence of virginity Cavendish's words; 'At home with my father a maiden he found me.'[30] Against Cavendish's statement, which was written by a man who detested her and was always willing to think the worst, must be balanced the opinion of the various foreign ambassadors who almost without exception reported rumours of sexual intercourse during the past six years. On top of this is the feeling of incredulity that anyone as virile as Anne and Henry could have manage chastity for six long years. Equally important but impossible to prove is sixteenth-century convention: most marriages did not take place until the woman had proved her fertility and become pregnant. This was especially important in an agricultural society where strapping young boys were needed on the farm and fathers were just as desperate for a male successor as the king. Henry's proposal of marriage back in 1527 did not mean that he was willing to undergo legal union without first proving the biological waters.

Anglici Matrimonij.

Sententia diffinitiua

Lata per sanctiss. inum . D.um Nostrum . D. Clementem . Pap5 . vij . in sacro Consissiorio de
Reuerendiss. morum Dominorum . S. R. E. Cardinalium consilio super validitate Matrimonij inter Serenissimos Henricum . VIII . & Catherinam Anglie Reges contracti.

PRO.

Eadem Serenissima Catherina Anglie Regina ,

CONTRA.

Serenissimum Henricum . VIII . Anglie Regem.

Clemens Papa. vij.

Hristi nomine inuocato in Trono iustitie pro tribunali sedentes, & solum Deum pre oculis habentes, per hanc
nostram diffinitiuam sententiam quam de Venerabilium Fratrum nostrorum Sancte Ro . Ec. Car. Consistorialiter
coram nobis congregatorum Consilio, & assensu ferimus in his scriptis, pronunciamus, decernimus, & declaramus,
in causa, & causis ad nos, & Sedem Apostolicam per appellationem, per charissimam in christo filiam Catherinam Anglie Reginam Illustrem a nostris, & Sedis Apostolice Legatis in Regno Anglie deputatis interposi
tam legitime deuolutis, & aduocatis , inter predictam Catherinam Reginam, & Charissimum in christo filium Henricum . VIII .
Anglie Regem Illustrem ,super Validitate, & inualiditate matrimonij inter eosdem Reges contracti, & consumati rebusq alijs in
octis, causa & causarum huiusmodi latius deductis, & dilecto filio Paulo Capissucho causarum sacri palatij tunc decano & pro
pter ipsius Pauli absentiam Venerabili Fratri nostro Iacobo Simonete Episcopo Pisaurien. vnus ex dictis palatij causarum Auditori
bus locumtenents, audiendis instruendis, & in Consistorio nostro Secreto referendis commissis, & per cos nobis , & eisdem Car
dinalibus Relatis, & mature discussis, coram nobis pendentibus, Matrimonium Inter predictos Catherinam, & Henricum An
glie Reges contractum , & inde secuta quecunq fuisse, & esse validum, & canonicum validaq, & Canonica , suosq debitos de
buisse, & debere sortiri effectus , prolemq exinde susceptam, & suscipiendam fuisse, & fore legitimam, & prefatum Henri
cum Anglie Regem teneri, & obligatum fuisse , et fore ad cohabitandum cum dicta Catherina Regina eius legitima coniuge , illamq
maritalis affectione , & Regio honore tractandum , & eundem Henricum Anglie Regem ad premissa omnia, & singula cum
effectu adimplendum condemnandum omnibusq iuris Remedijs cogendum , & compellendum fore , prout condemnamus,cogimus, &
compellimus , Molestationesq , & denegationes Per eundem Henricum Regem eidem Catherine Regine super inualiditate,ac se
dere dictis Matrimonij quomodolibet factas, & prestitas fuisse, & esse illicitas, & iniustas, & eidem Henrico Regi super il
lis ac inualiditate matrimonij huiusmodi perpetuum Silentium imponendum fore, & imponimus, eu.demq Henricum Anglie Re
gem in expensis in huiusmodi causa pro parte dicte Catherine Regine coram nobis , & dictis omnibus legitime factis condemnandum fore, & condemnamus , quarum expensarum taxationem nobis imposterum reseruamus.

Ita pronunciauimus .|.

Lata fuit Rome in Palatio Apostolico publice in Consistorio die. XXIII. Martij. M . D . XXXIIII .

Blosius.

12. Pope Clement VII's 'definitive sentence' in the debate over Henry's annulment of his marriage to Katherine of Aragon, finding in favour of his wife. This set the stage for Henry's defiance of Rome and decision to try the case in an English court where a decision favourable to the king was certain.

So far the scenario ignores Professor Bernard's argument that Henry, not Anne, was either responsible for commencing sexual relations in the fall of 1532 or for the earlier decision made sometime after 1527 to live dangerously and see if Anne would become pregnant. The question of responsibility is impossible to answer. What is easier to establish is the date of their marriage on 25 January 1533 that was determined by the announcement of Anne's pregnancy. The wedding had to be shrouded in absolute secrecy. There were still hopeful signs that the pope might even yet back down and grant the annulment, and he could not be allowed to be stampeded into a denial by hearing about the king's marriage. Moreover, and even more pressing, the pope had not yet confirmed the elevation of Cranmer to the archbishopric of Canterbury. Consequently, not more than a dozen people convened at the Holbein gate of Whitehall Palace in the pre-dawn to witness the king's defiance of papal authority. Henry was at his mercurial best; when asked by the officiating priest, probably Rowland Lee, later Bishop of Lichfield, whether he had the pope's license he answered yes knowing he possessed the papal bull allowing him to marry the sister of the lady who had been his mistress; technically not a lie but clearly not the literal truth. Wisely Henry had kept the ceremony small and brief. Those in attendance were mostly commoner and close friends, members either of Anne's or the king's privy chambers, and individuals who had few political axes to grind and could keep a secret.[31]

Pregnancy dictated the marriage timing but two previous events indicate that the king had been thinking about marriage and crowning his lover many months before his wedding. On Sunday 1 September 1532 in a marvellously ornate ceremony he created Anne Marquis of Pembroke in her own right (a very rare distinction) with an income of a £1,000 a year. Like most of the events in Anne's life the patent ennobling her is strangely defective. By omitting the customary words 'lawfully begotten' in describing her rightful heir, the patent made it possible for an illegitimate son to inherit the title. We have no idea whether the omission was a legitimate mistake or evidence that even at this late date Anne was still not certain of marriage. Elevated to the nobility Anne could now be displayed on the international stage and presented to Francis I of France. On 11 October Anne and Henry took ship from Dover for Calais accompanied by some 2,000 noblemen and a horde of servants, and throughout the week Anne was treated like a queen. This carefully and lavishly orchestrated display of wealth and honour was part of Henry's efforts to persuade Francis to acknowledge Anne as his bride. Francis was delighted to oblige because it assured him that Henry would make no secret alliances with Emperor Charles. Henry spent four days with his 'beloved brother' sovereign at the French court in the neighbouring town of Boulogne enjoying what was called a 'stag party'. Then Francis followed the English king back to Calais for four more days of dancing and feasting. Francis returned to France on 29 October after a wrestling display where the English champion prevailed. The whole affair had been an international engagement party with Anne as the bride. Now ennobled, she was well on her road to the throne.

13. Thomas Cromwell, indispensable to Henry VIII but low-born and only the son of a brewer and ironmonger. Coldly factual and analytical, he rose to be Principal Secretary, Vicar General in matters spiritual and Earl of Essex, but arranged the king's marriage to Anne of Cleves and was executed as a consequence.

Anne and Henry had planned to remain in Calais until 8 November but the fine weather turned vile and torrential storms kept them house-ridden until 10 November in makeshift accommodations in the Calais Exchequer. Their sleeping arrangements were certainly favourable to intimacy since Anne's bedroom connected to Henry's, and at least one historian has suggested this was the moment when the two finally slept together.

The ceremonial budget for 1532–3 must have been huge. Anne had been created Marquis of Pembroke in September with the full court in attendance and escorted by the Dukes of Norfolk and Suffolk. The Calais display took place in October and it was said to have cost the king at least £6,000. Then followed the Coronation in May only a week after the newly installed Archbishop Cranmer had annulled the king's marriage with Katherine, thereby freeing the king from bigamy. Some sources estimate that it cost Henry £46,000 to crown Anne Queen of England.[32] The process took four days, and started on Thursday 29 May with a regatta of some 200 vessels transporting the king and his wife from Greenwich to the Tower of London. Fifty barges, festooned with flags, bunting and gold foil carried the Lord Mayor, the London livery companies and Anne. The future queen was prominently displayed in the lead vessel, preceded by a mechanical device in the shape of a dragon spouting fireworks. With trumpets blowing and minstrels playing, 'the which were a right sumptuous and triumph sight to see and hear', the armada made its way to the Tower where Anne and her entourage stayed for forty-eight hours. Henry took the occasion for a magnificent display of chivalric pageantry when he created eighteen new Knights of the Bath and dubbed fifteen knights bachelor in ceremonies that lasted from Friday till Saturday.

The English social and political elite, both ennobled and commoners, turned out in force; the two most significant people missing without plausible excuses were the king's sister, Mary, Duchess of Suffolk and widowed Queen of France, who thoroughly disliked Anne both as a queen and a person for reasons never adequately explained, and Sir Thomas More, who had been given £20 by Bishops Tunstall and Gardiner to buy a new cloak for the Coronation. He kept the money but did not attend. It was a dangerous if highly principled decision; a year later he was a prisoner in the Tower.

No one has ever attempted to estimate the number of people who participated in Anne's Coronation but it must have been prodigious. The Venetian ambassador was vastly impressed by its 'very great pomp' and size, and noted what he called 'the utmost order and tranquillity' of the event. The weather was perfect but the twenty-first century, freed of sixteenth-century religious and social prejudices, cannot help but wonder about the logistics of the occasion; there must have been confusion aplenty and endless hurrying and waiting. The procession from the Tower to Westminster

Abbey was a half-mile in length and constantly paused at the multitude of pageants and sideshows performed along the way. It was scheduled to commence at 2.00 p.m. but did not start until 5 p.m. The nine royal judges on itinerant duty throughout the kingdom and representing the law's full endorsement of Anne as queen were ordered to march behind the gentlemen of the royal household but could not get to the Tower on time because of the crowds. They had to slip into place whenever they could as the procession moved by. The crowds along the procession route were dutifully enthusiastic, cheering and doffing their caps for Henry Tudor was popular as a man and as a monarch. How much of this loyalty rubbed off on his new wife is impossible to say, and there must have been plenty of silent ill-wishers in both the actors and audience. Those who could safely express their minds, like Eustace Chapuys, thought the occasion 'cold, meager and uncomfortable'; others noted that the crowds did little cheering, kept their caps firmly on their heads and laughed at the monogramming of the royal initials 'HA', transforming the spelling into 'ha ha'. Public displays and pageantry with their clash of colours and martial music were always popular in Tudor England and Henry had spent lavish sums of money to put on a magnificent performance. Most people were impressed and the new queen executed her exhausting role to perfection. The crowning took well over seven hours of elaborate ritual, during which the new queen was escorted by the Bishops of

London and Winchester, her train was held by the Dowager
Duchess of Norfolk, and the historic crown of St Edward
was set on her head by the Archbishop of Canterbury. It
was heavy and did not fit well and was soon replaced by a
lighter utilitarian version. High mass had to be performed,
offerings made, and the long walk back to the palace for
the wedding banquet in Westminster Hall, where its judges
and law clerks had been evicted for the occasion. The guests
numbered 800 of the most important people in the realm.
Anne sat at a marble table raised on a dais. She sat alone
except for the Archbishop of Canterbury who was seated at
her very far right. The new queen was situated in a marble
chair of state which was so uncomfortable that an inner chair
had been constructed for the feast, which must have lasted
hours for it included twenty-eight dishes for the first course
and twenty-four for the second and third. Cold food must
have been the common order of the day although the 800
guests were seated and fed according to their rank so there
was the possibility that the lesser people may have enjoyed
hot food if only because they were served fewer courses.
The Countesses of Oxford and Worcester stood behind
Anne holding a cloth to hide her face whenever she wanted
a semblance of privacy to spit, pick her teeth or blow her
nose. Two lesser ladies sat under the table to do her bidding.
The king meanwhile was seated in a box overlooking the
diners so he could view events in privacy.

The realm had done homage to its new queen, and her

relatives and friends were enjoying all the good things that accompanied the king's bounty. Friends and ill-wishers alike awaited the arrival of her child. Anne was six months pregnant. The king and ministers had done their best to introduce her to the kingdom, now it was up to Anne and God to do the rest and produce a legitimate male heir. Both signally failed in their assigned duty. To the 'great shame and confusion of physicians, astrologers, witches and wizards, all of whom affirmed that it would be a boy', the infant born at 3 p.m. on Sunday 7 September was Elizabeth Tudor.[33] Anne Boleyn had acquired the Tudor name and won herself a throne but she had failed in securing the male succession.

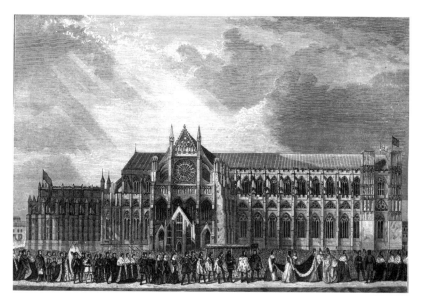

14. Anne's Coronation procession outside of Westminster Abbey. It may have cost Henry VIII the staggering sum of £46,000, but the king thought the money well spent.

6

Married to a King

Married to a king, Anne's life had consequences denied other wives. The operative word in the queen's story is 'catalyst', a person who precipitates a process or event without being involved in the consequences. Professor Ives however dismisses the word 'catalyst' entirely and substitutes the phrase a 'key element in the equation'.[1] Whether a catalyst or a key element, Anne Boleyn has the dubious distinction of having been a part of two such processes: the Protestant Reformation in England and the emergence under Henry VIII of the nation state. None of the four authors under review mention Anne's influence in the development of the nation state. Anne was a queen of many faces and the countenance that Ives likes best is of a strong-willed woman who knew her own mind and dictated her own terms. According to him, she 'played a major role in pushing Henry into asserting his headship of the Church'; she proved to be an adept politician by destroying the king's chief minister of almost twenty years; she helped conceptualise her sovereign's views of kingship; and as the wife of the monarch she acted as his much-needed alter ego.[2] As a consequence, she was, according to Ives, the godmother of English Protestantism, and it is clear that he agrees whole heartedly with a Scottish admirer of the lady who told Anne's daughter Elizabeth that 'true religion in England had its commencement and its end with your mother'.[3]

Not everyone will embrace Ives's assessment of the queen's role or importance to the growth of Protestantism but if his conviction that she was a sincere religious reformer and his speculation that she may have experienced 'a spiritual awakening' as a young adolescent in France are accepted, then his picture is an attractive one. He portrays her as something of an oxymoron, an evangelical but otherwise orthodox Catholic, deeply wedded to reading the Bible in the vernacular and almost a Protestant without realising it. One adoring observer of her taste for French books wrote that she was never without one in her hand and that he had 'seen her continually reading those helpful letters of St Paul which contain all the fashion and rule to live righteously'.[4] By implication the shades of Luther and Thomas Bilney are apparent but it is well to remember that Bilney did not die in the flames a Protestant, only a relapsed and rather idiosyncratic heretic. Erasmus, as already mentioned the most distinguished Christian humanist of his century, read and drew, like Anne, consolation from the Bible but never became a Lutheran. Nevertheless, Ives emphasises the religious gulf that he feels existed between the king, who was a friend of Erasmus and had also been influenced by Christian humanism, and his wife in their views on the role of faith in the attainment of salvation – 'when it came to personal religion, husband and wife were miles apart'. Ives notes that Anne's brother George may have been more radical than his sister.⁵ In his scaffold address George boasted that he had taken 'upon myself great labour to urge the king to permit the printing of the Scriptures to go unimpeded among the commons of the realm in their own language'.⁶ He translated, very likely at Anne's request, Lefèvre's biblical *Annotations*, writing, 'Believe, have faith, for without faith God doth not profit us, nor we can accomplish nothing,' which is not far from proclaiming Luther's justification by faith alone.⁷ The siblings were close both in taste and faith, and Anne carried with her in her final days in the Tower a French Bible the back cover of which read, 'The grace and truth is through Jesus Christ.' Given her devotion to the Bible in the vernacular, it is quite likely that Anne Boleyn was one of the many voices begging the king to allow the publication of Scriptures in English. The scene of Anne and Henry indulging in dinner conversations on religious subjects is well attested, and Scriptures must certainly have been among them.

Anne is often given credit for having befriended and promoted reformers who either became bishops during the years she was in power or became prelates under her daughter. In a number of cases she can take credit on the grounds that it happened during her administration but it is hard to find a case of promotion that did not have the king's approval. The cadre of divines that she gathered about her to be 'the lanterns and the light' of her household and to reprove her should she ever 'yield to any manner of sensuality'[8] were certainly reformers but not all of them ended up in the Protestant camp and two became important bishops under Catholic Mary. Queen Anne took seriously her duties to the poor and her charities were impressive but Retha Warnicke has warned, not very charitably, that much of this generosity can be explained as an effort to outdo the bounty of her arch-rival Katherine of Aragon. It was evidence of her royalty and spirit of competition, not her Christian faith.[9]

Where Eric Ives's portrait lacks substance is not the non-schismatic reform that Queen Anne promoted or her advocation of the crown's obligation to abolish clerical and monastic abuses now that Henry had assumed the supreme headship of the English Church but the lack of clear evidence that the queen was, in John Foxe's words, such 'a zealous defender of Christ's gospel all the world doth know, and her acts do and will declare to the world's end'.[10] The documentation simply does not exist, and Professor G. W. Bernard awaits to counter the story of Anne's so-called early Protestant crusade.

Bernard will scarcely give Anne credit for non-schismatic reform. He believes firmly that the king led in all matters spiritual and temporal and Anne dutifully followed. He accepts the queen as adopting ascetic Catholicism popular in the late medieval period but he will not embrace her as an evangelical Christian bordering on Protestantism either by conviction or policy. He denies that Cranmer was 'her man', puts a negative or conservative spin on much of Ives's evidence that Anne advanced crypto-Protestant divines, and paints the queen as a traditional Catholic who found understanding and consolation in the words of the Bible. He reminds his readers of Anne's all-important words to her jailer, spoken a few days before her execution – 'shall I be in heaven for I have done many good deeds in my day' – which brand her as an orthodox Catholic who believed in the power of good works. His most effective argument, however, to which Ives has no answer is her close association with John Skip, her almoner and divine on whom she called in her hour of need before her death. In April 1536, Skip preached a fiery and explosive sermon in the royal chapel with much of the king's council in attendance.[11] His first thunderbolt was directed at the king's councillors, whom he accused of being 'flatterers and deceivers' who only gave advice if they knew that the king was already 'deposed and incline to the same'. Rulers, he warned, must forever be on guard against the true and hidden motives of their councillors, and he bluntly accused the council of thievery: 'nowadays many men ... rebuke the clergy ... because they would have from the clergy their possessions'. He then branched out into a passionate defence of the Church of England and its ceremonies, and attacked critics who argued that smaller abuses were matters indifferent and therefore easily done away with as their justification for plundering the wealth of the ecclesia. Such advisers were hypocrites eager to denounce the whole Church for the sins of a single corrupt individual when they themselves were in fact far more debauched. He earmarked 'little ceremonies', such as holy water, palms, and holy ashes as being especially vulnerable. They were said to be meaningless relics of the past better abolished when in fact they were useful reminders of more profound Christian truths.

Ives spends just as much time on Skip's sermon as Bernard but for quite different reasons. They both claim the almoner's words were reflections of the queen's religious opinions and agree that if Skip were speaking for himself without Anne's permission and approval he would not have kept his position in her household. Ives, however, uses his words as evidence of the growing rift in the relationship between the queen and Thomas Cromwell, now the king's Vicar General in matters spiritual and in charge of the destruction of the monasteries. A very different and rather surprising Anne Boleyn emerges from Bernard's pages. Bernard cites Skip's close relationship with Anne to prove that she was no evangelical reformer but a conservative at heart voicing the doctrine of 'human prudence' – reform should never go so far that it damaged the Church which was the product of centuries of comfortable practice. That this was John Skip's message was displayed in his letter to Matthew Parker, later to be Elizabeth's Archbishop of Canterbury, written a year after Skip's elevation to the see of Hereford in 1539:

We of the Convocation, by reason of long absence from you, are decayed in quickness of wit, and so are become more dull and slow in our proceedings. Ye be hot and hasty: we be cold and tardy. We think that a great quantity of our qualities would do much amongst you, and a little portion of your qualities were enough for us. Ye be so prudent and expert in all things that ye need never to use deliberation though your matters were greater than they be, but we, for lack of your properties, are fain to respect and consult in all matters that we entreat of. Therefore, seeing this diversity between us and you, ye cannot blame us though we proceed diversely.[12]

Retha Warnicke's handling of the queen's religious preferences and activities are far blander than either Ives's or Bernard's and her conclusions more moderate but less interesting. She tries to accommodate both extremes, refusing to accept any alliance between Cromwell and Anne to promote religious radicals and agreeing with Bernard that Cromwell and the king did most of the promotion of bishops, but she accepts the queen as a dedicated reformer, and cautiously concludes that 'the two reformist issues she [the queen] is known to have favoured, the royal supremacy and scriptural translations, were supported by individuals as different as Hugh Latimer, [Thomas] Cranmer, [Edmund] Bonner, and [Nicholas] Heath...'[13] The first two became Protestant martyrs under Catholic Mary and the latter two her bishops who dutifully lit the fames. There is no better way to dramatise the difficulty in determining

Anne Boleyn's religious beliefs or in judging her part in the eventual triumph of Protestantism.

If the term catalyst is a matter of dispute in deciding Anne's role in the history of the English Reformation – both Ives and Bernard rejecting it for different reasons, one because it is not strong enough to describe her actions, the other because she did nothing to warrant the name – her association with the emergence of the nation state is even more tenuous because she was totally unaware of her impact, which nevertheless was overwhelming. Without Anne Boleyn the evolution of the nation state would have been fundamentally different. George Cavendish, writing under Catholic Mary and rejoicing that Anne's designs to advance her seed to the imperial throne had failed, still wrote the truth in his *Verses* when he had Anne claim, 'I was the author why laws were made' that built the nation state.[14]

The arrival of the nation state first in England, later throughout Europe, with its profound changes in the function and status of the individual in society, was an achievement that followed a path almost the opposite to that of the Reformation, which began as an event (Luther's Ninety-Five Theses) and ended in a process (Christian humanism). In contrast, the nation state commenced as a centuries-old process emerging out of the mist of the feudal past and culminated in four cataclysmic events all within twelve months of one another – the Act in Restraint of

Appeals, the Act of Supremacy, the Act of Treason and the Act of Succession, and all directly the consequence of Anne Boleyn's marriage to Henry VIII.

The essence of the nation state is an awareness of oneness and unity in which, as Bishop Bonner described it, the residents of the island community became conscious of a sense of Englishness, and 'in matters of State individuals were not to be so much regarded as the whole of the citizens'.[15] Once the peoples of England had transferred their many medieval allegiances from locality and immediate overlord to realm and king; and began talking about their island kingdom as that 'blessed isle', a spirit had been let loose that transformed a feudal conglomerate into a nation state. The spirit of nationalism subsumed all other loyalties, denied all other obligations, both local and international. By the early sixteenth century feudal disparity of language and politics had begun to give way to the monopoly of Anglo-Saxon as spoken by the citizens of London over both Latin and French and the incomprehensible dialects uttered in Yorkshire and Cornwall. A single language now proclaimed a single loyalty more demanding than that due to either nobleman or clergyman – fealty to the king. By Henry VIII's reign 'learned, unlearned, old and young, all understood the English tongue' and had begun to offer up their prayers to a monarch who must not only be obeyed but also worshipped as an idol. The eighth Henry, long before

Louis XIV of France gave words to the thought, believed and practised the doctrine '*l'Etat c'est moi*'.

Centuries before Henry absorbed papal power into his regal office, English kings had claimed dominion directly from God but that jurisdiction had to be shared with the divine authority of the overlord, priest, teacher, and father; all aspects of medieval power stemmed from God. By the sixteenth century, monarchs were beginning to grasp for sole power; Henry in the 1514 Hunne case had proclaimed in public that 'Kings of England have never had any superior but God alone', and 100 years earlier even the authority of the pope was being questioned. Pope Martin V bestowed a cardinal's hat on Bishop Beaufort of Winchester but failed to inform King Henry V, who angrily told the prelate that if he accepted the cardinal's hat, he would have no bishopric to go with it for he would be deprived of his see if he did so. Anti-papal feelings were running so high by the sixteenth century that the staunchly English Duke of Norfolk informed Cardinal Wolsey on the occasion of his appointment as papal legate that he gave not 'a straw' for the cardinal's legatine and foreign powers but that he honoured him because he was Archbishop of York, 'whose estate of honour surmounteth any duke now being within the realm'.[16] One of the most important attributes of medieval society, the existence of an international Church exercising direct authority from God and superior to any temporal jurisdiction, was on the wane, and Henry's defiance of Rome was simply the culmination.

Above: 15. Blickling Hall, Norfolk, where Anne was probably born. Most of the original fifteenth-century structure has been subsumed into this seventeenth-century residence.
Right: 16. Hever Castle, Kent, where Anne spent most of her childhood. Originally built in 1270 and turned into a manor house in 1462 by Anne Boleyn's great-grandfather, the building passed to Henry VIII on Anne's death and was given to Anne of Cleves as part of her divorce settlement from the king.

17. Sir Thomas Boleyn; he was elevated to the peerage as Earl of Ormond and Wiltshire but his reputation did not survive his role in accusing his son and daughter of adultery, incest and high treason. He died in his bed in 1539.

18. King's College statue of Henry VIII in all of his semi-divine magnificence, the undisputed regal heir to the red and white roses of the Lancastrian and Yorkist dynasties. Since Anne Boleyn married a divine-right sovereign, her life touched more intimately than most upon the sixteenth-century comprehension of the universe and royal divinity. *Opposite*: 19. Anne Boleyn as she may have looked when she first came to court in 1521; by her death in 1536 she had aged considerably and had become more like the shrew Catholic polemicists like to portray.

ANNA BOLLINA — UXOR HEN

Left: 20. Mary Boleyn, Anne's older sister and for a brief period mistress to Henry VIII. After the king tired of her she was married to William Carey, and their son Henry was often said to have been sired by the king. She was the only child of Sir Thomas to leave progeny for later generations.

Below left: 21. Henry VIII and Anne Boleyn's initials affectionately entwined at King's College Chapel, Cambridge. The initials during Anne's Coronation procession were mockingly turned into 'Ha Ha' by her ill-wishers.

Below right: 22. Henry VIII by Hans Holbein as he looked when he first fell in love with Anne Boleyn; a man of massive conscience.

Above: 23. An imaginative portrayal of Cardinal Wolsey learning that he had been fired from his office of Lord Chancellor. In October of 1529 he wrote an abject letter to the king craving 'grace, mercy, remission and pardon' and signing himself 'your Grace's most prostrate poor chaplain, creature and beadsman [humble petitioner]'.

Right: 24. William Warham, Archbishop of Canterbury, whose timely death in August 1532 removed one of the last barriers to the annulment of the king's marriage to Katherine of Aragon.

Theo. Moor L'Chancelour

Above: 25. Sir Thomas More, Henry's Lord Chancellor following the dismissal of Cardinal Wolsey. More was the most prominent humanist of his day, author of the *Utopia* and ardent persecutor of all varieties of heresy. His true character is still a matter of debate, but his execution in 1535 shocked the Christian world and turned Henry VIII into a barbaric monster as no other act did. Anne Boleyn received much of the blame.

Left: 26. Thomas Cranmer, the new Archbishop of Canterbury, who gave clerical blessings to the annulment of Katherine's marriage to the king. He was burned at the stake under Henry's very Catholic daughter, Mary Tudor.

Opposite: 27. Henry VIII's third wife, Jane Seymour, depicted here by Hans Holbein, died giving birth to his only legitimate son in October 1537.

KATHERINA VXOR HENRICI .. VIII.

Above: 28. The royal jousting yard where Henry is shown in full armour and on horseback tilting in front of Katherine of Aragon. In 1536 he was thrown from his horse and lay unconscious for two hours. It was his last joust and contributed to Anne Boleyn's miscarriage.

Centre left: 29. Katherine of Aragon, Henry VIII first wife and his brother's widow, *circa* 1520. She made a better martyr, suffering in silence, than opposition leader.

Below left: 30. Katherine of Aragon's grave in Peterborough Cathedral. She died of natural causes on 7 January 1536. With Katherine dead, Anne Boleyn realised that any third wife would be legally unimpeachable and her heir unquestionably legitimate.

31. The title page of Henry VIII's Great Bible in English depicting the proper structure of the king's new church in which Henry, as God's vicar on earth, dispenses divine truth to Thomas Cranmer and the clergy on his left and Thomas Cromwell and the laity on his right. At the bottom his grateful and dutiful subjects chorus '*vivat rex*', long live the king.

The break with Rome was central to the creation of the nation state for it went to the core of William Tyndale's preaching – 'One king, one law is God's ordinance' in every realm. 'All men without exception are under the temporal sword, whatsoever names they give themselves' was now a legal fact of Tudor life.[17] By the time that Anne Boleyn's marriage had been sanctified and legalised and her child named regal successor, the nation state had been fully shaped and instituted. The immediate need was to find a way to prevent Katherine from appealing her marital case to Rome as the highest spiritual authority in Christendom. Henry called upon parliament to legalise the principle that English law was without superior and that since Katherine lived in England and had in effect taken on English citizenship, the archiepiscopal court of Canterbury was the highest marital court of appeal in the land and no appeal could go further. No one seemed to recall that she was born Spanish, not English. The Act in Restraint of Appeals, however, went much further than denying the queen's ability to stop Henry from getting a legal annulment of their marriage, its first words set forth the principle of the sovereign independence of England:

> this realm of England is an empire, and so hath been accepted in the world, governed by one supreme head and king having the dignity and royal estate of the imperial crown of the same, unto whom a body politic … be bounden and owe to bear, next to God, a natural and humble obedience.[18]

Together the Acts of Supremacy and Restraint of Appeals heralded the advent of the modern leviathan, the sovereign national state. They not only turned the King of England into a pope in his own regal right but also presented a political creed that smashed forever the essential international duality of Christendom, divided into the two swords of Christ – the spiritual and the temporal. Caesar had won out over the Bishop of Rome in the struggle to monopolise God's representation on earth. The competition was as old as the Roman Empire but what was unique in sixteenth-century England was the organ through which Caesar voiced his will. As the pope spoke through and for the international medieval Church, so now the king spoke through and for the state. As the Church could do no wrong, so now the state claimed infallibility. The English people were confronted with the 'new found article of faith' that a statute made by the authority of the entire realm could not be thought to 'recite a thing against the truth'.[19] The moment the Act in Restraint of Appeals called England an empire and Henry assumed papal powers, the nation state was born.

With Katherine checkmated and legally divorced by an English court, with Anne Boleyn properly married to the king, and the principle of supremacy proclaimed, it was now time, the following year, to give his headship of the Church of England legal existence in the 'Act concerning the King's Highness to be Supreme Head of the Church of England' in 1534. The Act of Appeals took six pages to write, but the Act of Supremacy was drafted in only half a page because Convocation had already acknowledged the supremacy of the crown, and parliament was merely corroborating and confirming the same but without mention of the crucial phase 'as far as the law of Christ allows'. Henceforth Henry was to be

taken, accepted and reputed the only supreme head in earth of the Church of England called *Anglicana Ecclesia*, and shall have and enjoy annexed and united to the imperial crown of this realm ... all honours, dignities, preeminences, jurisdictions, privileges, authorities, immunities, profits and commodities, to the said dignity of supreme head of the same Church.[20]

Medieval kings had served as 'keepers of the peace and referees of civil behaviour'; Henry VIII had now become 'the ideological vicar' of his kingdom, whose duty was to mould public opinion and root out political and religious error.[21]

The great weakness of the Act of Supremacy was that it described the extent of the king's authority but said nothing about the punishments inflicted upon those who denied or infringed upon the principle. This was a defect taken care of in the new and extended Act of Treason passed within months of the supremacy Bill. The old treason law of 1352 suited the needs and spirit of feudal society, decreeing it treason to encompass the king's death, levy war against him, or help his enemies. Mere words were not construed as treason; an overt act had to be involved and proved. The new act brought the treason law up to date and gave legal safeguard to Henry's position as head of the Church. No medieval Englishman had ever thought of calling the king a heretic or schismatic or branding his children as bastards and incapable of inheriting the throne. More sweeping, the 1534 statute made treason by word of mouth punishable and stated that if anyone do maliciously wish, will or desire by words or writing, or by craft imagine, invent, practice or attempt any bodily harm to be done or committed to the King's most royal person, the Queen's or their heir's apparent, or to deprive them or any of them of the dignity, title or name of their royal estates, or slanderously and maliciously publish or pronounce, by express writing or words, that the King our sovereign lord should be heretic, schismatic, tyrant, infidel or usurper of the crown … [they] shall suffer such pains of death and other penalties as is limited and accustomed in cases of high treason.[22]

The word 'maliciously' blunted the law's teeth to a certain extent, and the law refrained from describing the gruesome penalty but Tudor England knew what awaited those who fell foul of the statute; they were tied to a hurdle and dragged to the place of execution, hanged for a short time by the neck, cut down while still conscious, castrated and disembowelled while still alive, and their bodies cut up and the pieces distributed for display throughout the kingdom.

One element was still missing; bodies could be mutilated to generate terror – as one monk put it, he acknowledged the king 'as supreme head for fear' but 'could not find in his conscience' to believe it[23] – but mind control was the surest safeguard of the king's supremacy and the new nation state. If the royal supremacy was to remain supreme and the realm safe from the papal dragon clamouring at the gates, Henry had to live and die by the words reported by John Foxe: his supremacy would 'lie post alone, hidden in the Acts of Parliament and not in the hearts of his subjects' unless he could reach into their souls and root out evil and seditious thoughts.[24] And so a new kind of loyalty oath was invented. In the Act for the Establishment of the King's Succession, passed in 1534 shortly after Anne Boleyn's daughter's birth, parliament, a secular body, pronounced that Katherine of Aragon's marriage to Henry was null and void, that his nuptials to his 'entirely beloved wife Queen Anne' should be taken 'for undoubtful, true, sincere and perfect ever hereafter', and finally that their lawful children should inherit the 'imperial crown', Elizabeth, the queen's daughter, being for the time the only heir. Five and a half pages later the act got down to the heart of the matter:

> all the nobles of your realm spiritual and temporal as all other your subjects [down to the village constable and priest] shall make a corporal oath ... that they shall truly, firmly and constantly without fraud or guile observe, fulfill, maintain, defend and keep to their cunning, wit and uttermost powers the whole effect and content of this present act ... and all other acts and statutes made since the beginning of this present parliament...

To refuse, to say 'that they be not bound to declare their thought and conscience', was high treason.[25]

32. Sir Thomas More and Bishop John Fisher escaped the terrible fate of the Carthusian monks – being drawn to the place of execution, hanged but cut down while still living, castrated and disembowelled – by execution reserved for the socially elite – the axe.

Oaths of fealty embracing loyalty to an overlord were the essential bonds holding feudal society together but the oath required by the Tudor state in 1534 was fundamentally different. It exacted not only acceptance of and obedience to but also approval of all statutes passed by the Reformation parliament, in other words, all aspects of the break with Rome and the king's supremacy. It was probably the first example of a modern loyalty oath, for example swearing that you had never been a member of the communist party. As Sir Thomas More complained, a subject was no longer 'bounden to the keeping' of the law; now he must 'swear that every law is well made'.[26] Despite Sir Thomas's and Bishop Fisher's defiance, the king achieved his purpose and all his subjects were expected 'to love, to obey and honour our prince not only outwardly in our bodies but also inwardly in our hearts, without any dissimulation or feigning'.[27] Conformity of mind now joined control of the body as instruments of maintaining unity and securing the nation state.

Sir Thomas More and Bishop John Fisher, though they escaped the grisly death reserved for traitors, lost their heads for refusing to take the 'corporal oath'. However, there were two other important figures of far greater concern and bitterness for Anne Boleyn who also refused the oath: Katherine of Aragon and her daughter, Mary Tudor. The relationship between Anne and her stepdaughter would today warrant a whole bevy of psychiatric conferences but in the sixteenth century it simply monopolised the attention and correspondence of the imperial ambassador, whose highly biased words have scripted their encounters and established the historical settings. Of the two, the daughter was the most dangerous to the new queen. Katherine was little more than a minor annoyance who could be sent away to her own abode as far away from court as Anne could persuade the king to arrange. Unfortunately, Henry still liked his first wife and wanted her around. Until he and Anne were actually married, Henry kept both ladies at court, used Katherine for ceremonial occasions, and actually dined when convenient with both of them together. Katherine could, however, still be strong-willed and obstinate as when she refused to lend Anne her daughter's ornate christening robe for the baby Elizabeth: 'God forbid that I should ever be so badly advised as to give help, assistance, or favour, directly or indirectly in a case so horrible as this.' In contrast, Princess Mary, now demoted to simply Lady Mary, was not only a delightful young girl of seventeen but worse, a permanent dynastic threat and the focus for all opposition to Anne.

What made Mary so potentially dangerous was a well-known and appreciated aspect of canon law; an infant born to a marriage thought by the parents to be legal remained legitimate even when the union had later been found to be invalid. Anyone conceived 'in good faith', as Mary surely was, could claim legitimacy, and in Mary's case could assert a better right to the throne than Anne Boleyn's own daughter, Princess Elizabeth. Only taking an oath acknowledging Elizabeth as heir apparent to the throne could negate Mary Tudor's birthright, and this she absolutely refused to do. For once Chapuys got it right when he reported Anne having said, 'She is my death, and I am hers.'[28]

33. The Lady or Princess, Henry VIII's elder daughter; the title depends on one's religious preference. She never got over the psychological trauma of being forced to publicly confess that her mother's marriage was 'incestuous and unlawful'. It is difficult to judge which of the two – Anne Boleyn or Lady Mary – was the more bloody-minded.

It is difficult to judge which of the two women was the more bloody-minded; the imperial ambassador was forever reporting that Anne was plotting to murder her stepdaughter and had actually said that should Henry leave the country to visit Francis of France and name her as regent in his absence, she would use her regental rights to order her execution for failing to take the oath of succession. If Anne could not manage that, she could have her starved to death. When Anne's brother George, now Viscount Rochford, suggested the king might be more than a little annoyed and her words were dangerously silly, she answered that she did not care what Henry thought even if she were burnt alive for her actions.[29] Chapuys was a fund of unlikely tales such as that Anne had persuaded an unnamed man to tell the king that he had had a revelation, presumably from God, that Anne could not conceive a male child while Katherine and Mary were still alive.

On her side Mary was almost as violent, not only refusing the oath but insulting Anne in public every chance she got. On one occasion when Anne was visiting the nursery of her daughter, where Mary Tudor had been forced to reside in the position of lady-in-waiting to the infant Elizabeth, the queen encountered her stepdaughter and ordered her to properly greet her as Queen of England. If she did so, Anne would arrange for more dignified accommodations. Mary refused to humble herself before the queen, saying she 'knew no queen in England other than her mother',

Katherine of Aragon, but she would be obliged if Anne could persuade the king to treat his elder daughter more kindly and with greater respect.[30] Two proud and obstinate women left the battlefield without either conceding an inch. Later orders came down from on high that Mary should no longer be served her meals by herself but must eat at the common table with the servants. Moreover, Lady Anne Shelton, Anne Boleyn's aunt and head of the nursery, was told to slap Mary Tudor's face ever harder each time she refused to refer to Anne as the queen or called herself a princess, 'being the cursed bastard that she was'.[31]

Anne was blamed by Chapuys for all of the harsh treatment inflicted upon Mary; the king is said to have been unaware of how beastly his wife was acting. This runs counter to two realities: Henry was determined that his daughter take the oath of succession and dutifully acknowledge her stepmother as queen and Elizabeth as Princess of Wales, and was set upon disciplining her as a disobedient child. Professor Ives is exceedingly loath to have his heroine take all the blame and her husband get off scot-free. There is little doubt that the king knew what was going on, although that statement along with so many other sentiments about Anne and the people around her is easier to state than prove. Henry, under Ives's pen from page twelve on of the biography, is presented as a weak sovereign who desired nothing but 'pastime with good company' and was a 'highly persuadable man'. Now, however, confronted with a mulish daughter, Ives presents the king in the character preserved in Holbein's famous painting – legs astride absolutely determined to stand his ground, bearing a massive body with an obstinate yet calculating face demanding imperious obedience from all his subjects. The sudden change in Ives's description of Henry's personality does not escape Professor Bernard's keen eye.[32]

If Chapuys can be believed, the presence of Katherine and Mary at court and Anne's obsessive fear that Henry would allow his fondness for his elder daughter to damage Anne's dynastic plans for Elizabeth were the central disputes undermining the marriage, although the presence of another young lady catching the king's fancy probably seemed a more pressing and immediate issue to the queen. What happened was that after two years of married life Henry reverted back to royal form, and the double standard existing between the sexes prevailed. Kings could have as many mistresses as they wanted but queens were forbidden lovers lest they place the succession to the throne in doubt. Anne was not always available for sex; she took time to recover from the birth of Elizabeth and then returned to her bed after a miscarriage, probably a male foetus. Henry's first wife had also spent much of her early married life incapacitated by pregnancies, and Henry could find no good reason not to take a mistress in the interims; Katherine had not objected, and he now expected the same understanding on the part of his new queen. Anne's reactions were not Katherine's long-suffering acceptance of her husband's infidelities. She ranted and raved and tried to arrange the expulsion of the young lady from court. Henry was not amused and informed her on one occasion 'she had good reason to be content with what he had done for her, which he would not do again if he were starting afresh' and 'she should remember where she had come from, and many other things'. On another juncture he ordered her to 'shut her eyes and endure just like others worthier than she' and that 'she ought to know that he could humiliate her in only a moment longer than it had taken to exalt her'.[33] Katherine's natural death on 9 January 1536 is said to have improved the marital atmosphere. Anne celebrated by dressing in yellow; Henry more properly mourned in black but privately rejoiced that the emperor would no longer be the family nemesis and support the pope's efforts to organise a Europe-wide crusade against the heretic English king. Moreover, Anne was once again pregnant, which pleased Henry immensely.

Ives cannot have his queen's marriage breaking up so soon and dismisses the sudden presence of mistresses as natural to orthodox kingship. By the standard of the century Henry had a right to be irritated at his wife's oversensitivity; her trouble was that she was not to royalty born, and did not understand. This kind of family friction is treated as yet another example of a lover's quarrel, and

Ives refuses to 'attach too much importance to it' since 'Henry was so fickle and Anne knew how to manage him'.[34] In this case he may be correct, at least until Anne's second miscarriage on 29 January 1536.

7

Miscarriage to Execution:
Four Versions

So far the squabbling among Anne Boleyn's biographers over her character and behaviour have been more about degree and form than about substance. Now, both the flavour and intensity of the debate change dramatically, heating up, as they differed over the substance and cause of what actually occurred during the last weeks of the queen's life. Each author deserves serious attention as each develops very different interpretations of the king's actions and the need for the queen's execution.

Eric Ives
The Life and Death of Anne Boleyn

Eric Ives is a faithful disciple of Paul Friedmann in that both authors cast Thomas Cromwell as the *deus ex machina* of the plot, the only person who knew what was going on and why. They differ dramatically, however, in their estimate of the central character. For Ives, Anne Boleyn is the perfect heroine, one of only two queen consorts who ever 'married for love'; for Friedmann, 'Anne was not good; she was incredibly vain, ambitious, unscrupulous, coarse, fierce and relentless'.[1] Possibly both evaluations are partially correct.

Ives commences the narrative of Anne Boleyn's final months by introducing Jane Seymour, Henry's future and third wife, into the plot. Henry and Anne were on a late-summer progress through Wiltshire in 1535 and stopped for a week at the Seymour residence of Wolf Hall. Whether Jane was there is unknown but by February of the following year she was Anne's recognised rival at court and her brother Edward was a rising courtier just invited into the king's Privy Chamber. Jane herself had been a lady-in-waiting to Katherine of Aragon and performed the same duties for Queen Anne. Jane came from a family of ten children; it was not her good looks, which were reportedly not great, that attracted Henry but the fecundity of her clan. He was thinking of a new and fertile wife.

It was hard times for almost everybody, plague, taxes, the smaller monasteries were being closed and their wealth confiscated, the international configuration seemed to predict a papal-led crusade against the heretic King of England, and in January Henry was thrown from his tilting steed and was unconscious for two hours. The single exception to this picture of gloom was Anne Boleyn, happily pregnant again with what she felt to be Henry's much-desired male heir.

Two events profoundly changed both the domestic and

foreign scenes: Katherine of Aragon died on 7 January 1536, and Queen Anne miscarried her male child twenty-two days later on the 29th. She blamed the emotional shock of Henry's jousting accident and the sight of Jane Seymour sitting on the king's lap as the causes of the miscarriage of what indeed was a 3½-month-old male foetus. Ives spends several pages dismissing the story that the foetus was misshapen or deformed, and downplays the allegedly 'absolute secret' words of the Marquis and Marchioness of Exeter that Henry had confessed that his marriage had been 'seduced and constrained by sortileges [divination and/or witchcraft] and for this reason he held the said marriage void and that God had demonstrated this in not allowing him to have male heirs, and that he considered that he could take another'.[2] Since the source of these words came from the imperial ambassador, neither secrecy nor accuracy could be relied on at Henry's court. In Ives's view the theory that the foetus was the product of witchcraft is 'a mountain of fancy' and Henry's fear that his marriage was seduced and constrained by witchcraft is nonsense never mentioned at Anne's trial.

Anne's miscarriage, however, must have been a profound shock to a father who invariably looked for someone outside himself to blame; Henry picked up where he had left off with Katherine; God was telling him something, and his only words to his wife were, 'I see that God will not give me male children.' The crucial question was why? Ives feels that

Anne's position was not as dire as often depicted; she was no worse off after the miscarriage than before she got pregnant, and he dismisses as grossly overdramatic Sir John Neale's oft-quoted words that 'she had miscarried her saviour'. She was certainly vulnerable. Mary Tudor remained a threat and Jane Seymour was a dangerous contrast to Anne: in Ives's words 'fair, not dark; younger by seven or eight years; gentle rather than abrasive; of no great wit, against a mistress of repartee; a model of female self-effacement, against a self-made woman'.[3]

The conservative interests, essentially the core of the Plantagenet party that had been a powerful faction when Anne first came to court and was delighted in 1536 to use any means to get rid of her, began to cultivate Mistress Seymour the moment the king started to eye her as something more than a partner in the ritual of courtly love while Anne was heavy and clumsy carrying her child. They tried to train her in how best to attract the king and hold his attention. In so doing they drew on Anne Boleyn's own past experiences. Jane was an apt pupil, and when Henry sent her a purse full of gold coins and a letter she returned both unopened to the messenger saying that she was

a gentlewoman, born of good and honourable parents and with an unsullied reputation. She had no greater treasure in the world than her honour which she would rather die a thousand times than tarnish, and if he wanted to give her money she begged that he would do so once God had sent her a good match.

To the question of why she did not open the king's letter, Ives proposes the answer that she already knew what was in it – 'a summons to the royal bed'.[4] Henry was said to have been deeply touched by such a display of modesty.

The presence of a newly trained and refurbished Jane Seymour was not the only critical factor in the months after January 1536; the queen's quarrel with Thomas Cromwell, according to Professor Ives, was far more serious. The issue was the fate of the smaller monasteries that Cromwell and the king had managed to have parliament dissolve and whose wealth they had confiscated. The original justification for this legislation was that the lands and riches of these allegedly corrupt and useless institutions were better spent on educational and charitable causes. It soon became clear, however, that Cromwell and his king wanted the money to go into the royal exchequer to finance the royal supremacy, not to endow new colleges at Oxford and Cambridge; Anne and many others strenuously objected. John Skip's sermon against rapacious councillors bent on plundering the Church is presented as evidence of the growing rift between the queen and Vicar General. The Dissolution Bill, which included the right of the crown to reprieve any monastery it wanted to, had passed parliament in March but still required the king's signature. According to Ives, with Anne's ability to manipulate her husband and the king's pliability, Cromwell's goal of closing all the smaller monasteries was still very much in jeopardy, and he was deeply disturbed.

Through February and March, Henry was surprisingly loyal to his Boleyn marriage, especially so after the death of Katherine and the end of Emperor Charles's assertion she was the legitimate Queen of England. The king was insistent that the emperor now recognise and support his marriage and accept Princess Elizabeth as his legal heir. With the late queen out of the picture, a diplomatic revolution seemed to be in the making with England and the Habsburg Empire once again allied. In demanding imperial recognition for his marriage and acknowledgement that the papal refusal to grant him an annulment was wrong, Henry was imposing upon diplomatic negotiations impossible terms, and he was at serious odds with his entire council and especially with Thomas Cromwell, who had decided that friendship with Charles V was essential to the country's welfare.

The picture of the king stubbornly at war with his council fits badly the image of Henry as a weak and easily influenced monarch so essential to Ives's thesis. Ives never admits the contradiction but clearly senses that Henry is not behaving according to form. He attempts to resolve the dichotomy and at the same time supply Cromwell with a motive for plotting Anne's destruction by claiming that in the Vicar General's eyes Anne was the guilty party, exerting her dangerous influence over the king and urging him on to make impossible demands on both Charles and the French king. He not only asserts that Cromwell thought her responsible for the diplomatic impasse but also that she was behind the growing and serious opposition to the Dissolution of the Monasteries and could easily persuade Henry to exempt a host of monasteries from dissolution. For Cromwell it all added up to a single conclusion: Anne must go; she imperilled the country and Cromwell's career. This is a clever hypothesis, but, alas, there is not an ounce of historical evidence that Anne ever tried to control Henry's diplomatic policies or that Cromwell believed she did. It is all surmise, possibly true, but totally unproven.

The timing of events is baffling and highly confusing, so much so that it looks as if Henry were destroying and supporting his queen all on the same day, 24 April, signing the commission of Oyer and terminer to investigate and charge Anne and her five suspected lovers with treason, and at the same time negotiating with both Charles V and Francis I of France to support the Boleyn marriage. Ives does away with the confusion by having Cromwell, not the king, responsible for initiating and signing the commission. This allowed time for him to manufacture a crisis of sufficient magnitude to drive (Ives calls it bouncing) Henry out of his pro-Boleyn stance. Up until 25 April the king was still referring to Anne as 'our most dear and most beloved wife'.

Ives finds his crisis in what he describes as a major dispute between Anne and Sir Henry Norris, the groom of the stool and head of the king's Privy Chamber. Presumably the encounter was well known in court circles long before Anne reported it to Sir William Kingston, her jailer at the Tower of London and one of the few reliable sources for Anne's final days. It began when the queen asked Norris why he was delaying his marriage to Anne's cousin Margaret Shelton; she suspected Norris's hesitancy reflected the declining political influence of the queen and her party at court. Norris's unrecorded answer provoked Anne into 'a shocking imprudence'. She said, 'You look for dead men's shoes; for if ought came to the king but good you would look to have me.' Norris, quite properly was horrified by the implications of Anne's words, which were tantamount to planning the king's death and remarriage for Anne. Norris swore 'he would his head were off' rather than think such treasonous thoughts. Then, again according to Ives, 'a right royal quarrel about their relationship' ensued.[5] Who told the king is never divulged but a few days later Anne and Henry certainly had a first-class row about something, conceivably about his wife and her relations with his best friend and favourite competitor on the tennis court and tilting yard. Cromwell then fuelled the king's anger by bringing to the king's attention Mark Smeton's confession that he had slept with the queen three times. By the night of Anne's arrest on 2 May Henry was in tears, telling his illegitimate son, the Duke of Richmond, 'that he and his sister [Mary] owed God a great debt for having escaped the hands of that cursed and poisoning whore who had planned to poison them'.

Ives expands Cromwell's plot against the queen into a full-scale political attack upon her court faction, Sir Henry Norris and George Boleyn, the queen's brother, Viscount Rochford, being Cromwell's most dangerous political enemies. Sir Francis Weston, a particularly handsome young gentleman of the king's Privy Chamber, who like Norris had visited the queen's quarters too often for his safety, was included in the mix in order to conceal the fact that the plot was in reality not an action to punish an adulterous queen but a 'sordid factional putsch'. As for William Brereton, how he got on the Principal Secretary's list of adulterous lovers remains unclear. Ives resolves the matter by saying that 'he was picked on as an act of gratuitous malice (or perhaps rough justice), following an earlier and quite separate altercation with Cromwell'.[6]

The queen's brother was not only accused of adultery but also incestuous intercourse with his sister. It is also possible that he and Anne laughed together at the king's sexual ineptitudes, his occasional impotency, his style of dress and clumsy poetic verse. George Boleyn was an easy man to bring down and it was easy to find colleagues willing to debase his character; he was outspoken, scornful of others and overly proud of his many talents.

Of Anne Boleyn's five named paramours only Mark Smeton remains unexplained. He was the first to be arrested, the only one to confess to actually entering the queen's bed, and the only one to have his story vastly improved in the telling. Mark was a young, extremely well-paid Flemish musician in the king's chambers, gifted at the lute and virginal, a graceful dancer and a marvellous singer. He liked to display his talents and lived well beyond his means, sufficient to purchase three expensive horses and rich livery for his servants. He aspired to be a gentleman yet clearly wasn't, and the assumption that he had other sources of income, possibly from the queen, led to dangerous gossip. He grew very grand in his ways and arrogant in his associations, and the dislike that he generated among his equals led to Cromwell learning that he was a favourite of the queen and worthy of close interrogation. Whether he was tortured to extract his confession is unknown but suspected, and in the *Spanish Chronicle* 'pulp fiction' version of what happened, a rope was tied around his skull, tightened agonisingly to force the revelation of an affair with the queen that reads like the purest creative fantasy. Anne is cast as the nymphomaniac aggressor who arranges to have Mark smuggled into her chambers. He was hidden naked in the sweetmeat closet in the anteroom to Anne's bedchamber and was available whenever she called out the code word, 'marmalade'. With the queen's sex life reduced to a citrus preserve, Ives makes it clear that he would prefer to be dealing with less fatuous tales.[7]

A less apocryphal story has to do with George Boleyn's wife, who uncharitably testified against her husband, reporting 'there was a familiarity between the queen and her brother beyond what so near a relationship could justify'. This was the genesis of the charge of incest and is part of the inspiration for the suggestion that George was homosexual, a fiction that Ives dismisses 'out of hand' as nonsense. Equally unacceptable are the words of Lancelot de Carles, the poetry composer in the French embassy, who puts both Norris and George Boleyn in bed with the queen and has Henry being informed, 'When at night you retire, she has her toy boys already lined up. Her brother is by no means last in the queue. Norris and Mark [Smeton] would not deny that they have spent many nights with her without having to persuade her, for she herself urged them on and entangles them with presents and caresses.' Ives is adamant; 'this is moonshine'.[8]

A jury of twenty-six peers of the realm, with the Duke of Norfolk presiding, was convened not to do justice but, without a dissenting voice, to find Anne and her 'lovers' guilty. With the exception of Mark Smeton they all denied the charges and pleaded not guilty, Anne swearing even as she took mass that she was innocent and a faithful wife to the king. According to one chronicler, she 'made so wise and discreet answers to all things laid against her, excusing herself with her words so clear as though she had never been faulty to the same'.[9] Ives accepts the ring of truth in Carles's report of Anne's concluding speech to the court: 'I do not say that I have always borne towards the king the humility which I owed him, considering his kindness and the great honour he showed me and the great respect he always paid me: I admit, too, that often I have taken it into my head to be jealous of him … but may God be my witness if I have done him any other wrong.'[10]

The indictment against Anne is effectively demolished as nonsense. Three quarters of the allegations are easily disproved and in twelve of the cases against her either the queen or the partner involved was elsewhere than claimed. The oft-repeated phrase, 'treasonably violated the queen', becomes meaningless when confronted with Anne's alleged consent. Moreover, adultery with the queen was not a treasonous offence. That twenty-seven noblemen found them all guilty has bothered observers ever since, including the imperial ambassador, who had no love for Anne; he said she was 'condemned on presumption and not evidence, without any witnesses or valid confession'. Ives has little good to say of anyone involved in the queen's destruction but he is strangely tolerant of Thomas Cromwell if he really was the brains and manipulator behind what is portrayed as judicial murder. Ives's venom is reserved for the king, who is condemned for washing his hands of the whole disgusting affair and at the same time accused of displaying 'nauseous' interest in arranging for a French executioner to kill his wife. It cost the crown £23 6s to hire the expert, an exorbitant sum.

In one area alone is there full agreement. All five of the victims died well by the standards of their age, and Anne died magnificently by any standards. Her age called her performance 'bold' because she in fact never confessed to any crime. She proclaimed,

> Good Christian people, I have not come here to preach a sermon; I have come here to die. For according to the law and by the law I am judged to die, and therefore I will speak nothing against it. I am come hither to accuse no man, nor to speak of that whereof I am accused and condemned to die, but I pray God save the king and send him long to reign over you, for a gentler, nor a more merciful prince was there never, and to me he was ever a good, a gentle, and sovereign lord. And if any person will meddle of my cause, I require them to judge the best. And thus I take my leave of the world and of you, and I heartily desire you all to pray for me.[11]

G. W. Bernard
Anne Boleyn: Fatal Attractions

Like any well-trained strategist, Professor Bernard does not reveal his argument until he has successfully demolished all possible opponents and their fallacious theories. He starts with Retha Warnicke's contention that Anne's fall resulted from a deformed foetus in the queen's miscarriage of 29 January. It led Henry to accuse his wife of having used witchcraft in holding him to his marriage because everyone knew that a malformed foetus was a sure sign that Anne was a witch and had practised illicit and libertine sex before conceiving such a horror. Bernard denies that there is any hard evidence of malformation All we have is the vague and highly prejudiced musings of Nicholas Sanders, a Catholic polemicist, writing two generations after the event, and describing the undeveloped foetus as 'a shapeless mass of flesh'. On the other hand, reports exist that Anne gave premature birth to a perfectly normal boy child at least twenty weeks early. Having dismissed the theory of a deformed foetus, Bernard then asks the sensible question of why, if Anne were a practising witch, did she permit the miscarriage of what was so obviously her 'saviour'? A more answerable question is to ask why, despite the evidence against it, has the story of witchcraft and a malformed foetus been so persistent over the years? Its attraction seems to lie in the fact that it offers a possible explanation how and why five men got tied into Henry's efforts to do away with a wife who seemed to be unable to supply him with any more children, let alone a male heir.

As the story is told, if Henry's miscarried son was grotesquely shaped it had to be Anne's fault; it was unthinkable that a king who spoke to God could have been responsible. Since miscarriages were said to be punishment for excessive nymphomaniac sex beforehand, Anne must have had a plethora of lovers who had to be found and punished along with the queen, thereby relieving Henry of all culpability. As Bernard observes, this scenario turns the king into an ignominious and impotent cuckold. Professor Bernard is not impressed; in his estimation 'any man would regard his impotence and his wife's adulteries as far more humiliating than any deformed foetus'.[12] Moreover, as both Bernard and Ives point out, neither the misshapen foetus nor witchcraft ever appear in the indictment against the queen, and if they were as central as Warnicke makes them, they would have been used against Anne during her trial.

Having removed bell, book and candle from the plot, Bernard deconstructs another favourite legend about Henry VIII, that he was an oversexed Lothario going through women like some men go through socks. The number of the king's mistresses was not excessive by the standards of his age and was downright minuscule compared to the sexual activities of his brother sovereign, Francis I of France, whose love-life was the talk of Europe and who actually did die of syphilis. In fact, Henry was a rather prudish man. Bernard also downplays Henry's obsession for a male heir to save his kingdom from civil war. Henry Tudor, it is often said, was not only willing to divorce Katherine of Aragon but also risk his immortal soul by defying the spiritual head of Christendom for the sake of male heir and a peaceful succession. Bernard finds the logic unacceptable: 'A king anxious about the future of his realm would not have embarked on the [politically dangerous] divorce that Henry pursued, much less the break with Rome.'[13] Obviously Bernard does not regard Henry's much-heralded conscience as being sufficient inducement.

Bernard admits that the succession could have been the driving force behind some of the king's actions. The birth of a daughter in 1533, not a son, and the tragedy of two other miscarriages 'can readily be seen as pushing Henry over the edge and causing him to resolve to ditch Anne'.[14] Such an easy explanation, however, runs afoul of the king's attachment to his Boleyn marriage right up to a week before his wife's arrest, three months after the 29 January miscarriage. Interestingly, Professor Bernard does not comment either in his text or footnotes that Professor Ives wrestled with and in part resolved this problem six years before Bernard put pen to paper. The two professors, however, are agreed that the queen continued to have the king's trust for months after the miscarriage. Their only difference being Bernard's use of stronger language: as late as 18 April [Ives says 25 April] Anne was 'totally secure in the king's favour'.[15] He also feels that the speed with which Henry was formally engaged to Jane Seymour on the day after Anne's execution and was married on 30 May are in no way arguments that the king or anyone else secretly felt Anne to be innocent. Instead the king's hasty remarriage reflected 'his need to cover the shame of what Anne had allegedly done to him by committing adultery, and maybe even more humiliatingly, in talking about his impotence'.[16]

An antithesis remains – Anne was the victim of factional rivalry and a political plot to get rid of her was arranged by either the conservatives at court or the king's chief minister, Thomas Cromwell, or by an alliance of the two. The symbolic heads of the conservative party were the demoted Queen Katherine and her daughter Lady Mary who, Bernard points out, were not very effective leaders. Katherine was by instinct a far better martyr, suffering in silence, than a political organiser, and her daughter Lady Mary was too young and inexperienced to do anything except take orders. As an organisation the conservatives consisted of the old Plantagenet faction plus a few key members of the king's Privy Chamber, in particular Nicholas Carew. Most of the evidence of their existence is supplied by the indefatigable imperial ambassador, who is rarely a credible witness. As Bernard wisely observes, a political party plotting a coup is more than just a list of names, and that 'the danger of the conspiratorial approach to history is that it drives the would-be unmasker of plots into a world of speculation in which "must have" and "surely" do duty for evidence'.[17]

This leaves Thomas Cromwell as the mastermind behind Anne's destruction. Presumably he had his own political agenda for destroying the queen and successfully poisoning the king's mind by concocting evidence of her incest and adultery. According to the conspiracy theory proponents, Cromwell achieved a 'double reversed twist, ridding himself of Anne first, with the support of Mary and her allies, and then ditching them too'; the hallmark of a master politician.[18] The scheme looks good on paper but Bernard asks why, if the conservatives played such an important role in the queen's fall, did the destruction of the monasteries and the attack on Church ceremonies and images continue unabated; and why was Lady Mary compelled to accept her father as Supreme Head of the Church of England well after Anne's death?

Nor can Bernard find any tangible reason for Cromwell to regard the queen such a powerful political enemy that she had to be destroyed. One hypothesis has Anne's opposition to the destruction of the monasteries for crass monetary reasons as the basis for Cromwell's concern; surely a quick growl from a sovereign, who was the divine head of the Church, would have ended all opposition. If nothing else Anne was a dutiful subject and wife of a divine-right monarch. Another theory argues that Anne was a diplomatic burden, interfering with the king's chief minister's efforts to take advantage of Katherine of Aragon's death and renewal of the old alliance between Emperor Charles V and the supreme head of England with his schismatic Church. Bernard goes to the root of the problem when he poses the question, 'would a king's leading councillor invent false charges of incest with her brother' and adultery with five men, simply because he favoured an alliance with the emperor and she did not? 'It betrays a lack of proportion.'[19]

The entire plot lacked proportions, and Bernard asks why did the crime have to be incest and adultery and include five men; why not theft or embezzlement and only one or two people involved? Bernard objects to turning Cromwell into a Machiavellian villain, who uses monstrous means to achieve easily attainable ends. Equally mysterious, the men brought down with Anne did not 'constitute an obvious faction' nor were they all Cromwell's political rivals.[20] Mark Smeton was a musician with no political influence, Francis Weston was young and new to court and only knighted during the Coronation ceremonies in 1533. He was a lesser member of the king's Privy Chamber, played tennis and bowls with his sovereign, and came from a wealthy family. George Boleyn, Viscount Rochford, had political ambitions but as yet was a relatively minor player who possessed a biting and witty tongue that earned him a host of enemies. Sir Henry Norris as chief of the Privy Chamber might be described as a political rival but Bernard says there is 'little to suggest that Norris was at all interested in political matters'.[21] In truth there is little to say he was not interested in politics either. Both Norris and William Brereton may have been causing trouble for Cromwell in his efforts to modernise and extend the nation state into the ancient feudal Marcher lordships of Wales by standardising the king's authority and introducing sheriffs and shires into the Welsh mountains. Norris and Brereton had been granted extensive lordships throughout the region, which they profitably ruled with iron hands, but they could have been dismissed with a gesture by the king with no need for adultery.

One awkward document remains, a description by Chapuys of his conversation with Cromwell in which the king's chief minister says '*a fantasier et conspirer le dict affaire*', roughly meaning 'I invented and plotted the whole affair'. The ambassador also reported that Henry had said to the Bishop of Carlisle that 'it was already a good while that he had been aware of the likely outcome of these matters'.[22] Bernard clearly believes that Cromwell was bragging and is taking credit for a lucky situation that had removed a number of his political rivals and potential enemies from the scene. Cromwell had nothing to do with fabricating the story of the queen's adultery, but once the story of her actions in her bedchamber emerged he took full advantage of it and organised the government's case against Anne and her alleged lovers. Henry was fully informed about the accusations that stemmed from something quite different from a political plot.

All the solutions offered to explain Anne's fall – her failure to conceive a male successor to the throne, Henry falling in love with another woman, political factions determined to destroy her, Cromwell acting as the mastermind of political murder – all share a single assumption; Anne and her so-called lovers were innocent of adultery and plotting the king's death. Bernard now reveals his explanation: 'It will now be suggested that Anne and at least some of those accused with her were guilty of adultery.'[23]

Lancelot de Carles's epic poem written either during the drama or immediately afterwards is the critical document because it not only names the protagonists but tells how the story of Anne's sexual activities came to light and was reported to the king. It all started with a quarrel between Sir Anthony Browne, one of the king's councillors, and his sister, the Countess of Worcester, the lady who stood behind the queen holding the napkin that supplied a modicum of privacy during the Coronation banquet and who was one of the ladies of the queen's chamber. The countess was clearly pregnant but her husband was out of town and might not have been the father. Sir Anthony wanted an explanation. His sister gave as an answer that all sorts of lovemaking went on in the queen's chambers and if her brother thought she was sleeping around it was not anywhere near as extensive or dangerous as Anne's activities, which included Mark Smeton, Sir Henry Norris and her brother George Boleyn. Sir Anthony was caught between the devil and deep blue sea; to conceal treason warranted the death penalty, but to report false and defaming information about the queen was also treason. He consulted two colleagues and they advised informing the king. They named Smeton, George Boleyn and Norris; Henry ordered an investigation and within twenty-four hours Anne and all the others were in the Tower of London, Weston and Brereton having been added to the list by information supplied by Smeton. Bernard concludes in oddly negative phraseology that 'it is hard to see why the essentials of de Carles's poem should be disbelieved'. He refuses to accept Ives's hypothesis that de Carles in his poem was simply quoting information that Cromwell had already fed the French ambassador that was all fabricated from the start. Several sources name the Countess of Worcester as the origin for the allegations against the queen, and Bernard is satisfied as to 'how and why Henry should have found the charges against Anne plausible, and ordered her arrest'.[24]

34. The Tower of London by Anthony van Wyngaerde. Originally built by William the Conqueror, the Tower was a fortress, prison, royal residence and repository for the state archives, but most of all it was a symbol of royal authority where two of Henry's wives were executed.

Anne's words to Sir William Kingston, her jailer while in the Tower, added coffin nails to the case that the government, largely in the form of Cromwell's organisational skills, was building against her. She revealed the quarrel with Norris and their conversation about 'dead men's shoes' and 'if anything came to the king you would look to have me'. She had given the government proof of plotting the king's death.[25] She also inadvertently sealed Francis Weston's fate by telling Kingston about a conversation with the young man in which he said 'he loved one in her house better than them both', meaning his wife and mistress, Anne's cousin, Margaret Shelton. When Anne asked who was the third lady, he answered, 'It is yourself.' She scolded him but the harm was done, allowing Cromwell to interpret the words as he desired. Bernard admits that the queen's remarks in the Tower in no way proved adultery but he claims that they certainly admit of the possibility. As he says they were 'inappropriate for any married woman, and *a fortiori* for a queen'.[26]

Bernard is not bothered by the fact that three-fourths of the government's indictments, naming the dates and places of the alleged adulteries, can be refuted as physically impossible because there were never any eyewitnesses *in flagrante delicto*, and no one took the charges as anything more than lawyer-talk. More dangerous was the 'catch-all phrase' referring to 'various other dates and places' which was an accusation much more difficult to deny for it offered no dates to be refuted and denied. The weakest point of Bernard's thesis is difficulty explaining away Anne's magnificent performance on the scaffold where she confessed to nothing, and no one has disproved her many and passionate acclamations of innocence. His only response is to indulge in character assassination, listing the innumerable cases where people had described Anne as a whore and a harlot, all of which have the ring of overkill to them. His digging up of the old sexual scandals with Henry Percy, Earl of Northumberland, and Thomas Wyatt come close to slander.

More effective is his handling of Anne's alleged bedmates. He starts by using Thomas Wyatt and Richard Page's brief incarcerations in the Tower and their eventual release, and Francis Bryan's interrogation as proof of the legitimacy of the investigation against them all: the innocent were set free. Mark Smeton he feels was guilty and spent at least three nights with the queen as he confessed. He dismisses as unfounded speculation that Smeton was also George Boleyn's homosexual lover. He gives her brother George and Brereton somewhat reluctant clean bills of sexual health; Brereton because he was over fifty and fell victim to unpopularity as a man whose past life might well have deserved death; the viscount because incest was unlikely in and of itself and impossible to prove. What earned George the death penalty was his having, according to Chapuys, laughed one evening with Anne about the king not being 'physically capable of copulating with women and that he had neither virtue nor power' to do so, and having publicly spread doubts about the paternity of Princess Elizabeth.[27]

Francis Weston remains high on the suspicion list largely because of his scaffold address in which he admitted, 'I had thought to have lived in abomination yet this twenty or thirty years and to have made amends,' and the letter he wrote his parents in which he begged special forgiveness from his wife.[28] Next to Smeton, Henry Norris, despite his refusal to confess and receive from the king a pardon, is Bernard's prime candidate as Anne's long-term lover. Bernard gladly accepts that a number of the accusations could have been the result of misunderstandings about what actually happened, but he concludes that it is just 'my own hunch that Anne had indeed committed adultery with Norris, probably Smeton, possibly with Weston, and was then the victim of the most appalling bad luck when the Countess of Worcester, one of her trusted ladies, contrived in a moment of irritation with her brother to trigger the devastating chain of events that led inexorably to Anne's downfall'.[29] In other words, one of those extraordinary coincidences that no one in the sixteenth century ever believed in and found quite impossible.[30]

Retha M. Warnicke
The Rise and Fall of Anne Boleyn

Retha Warnicke has become the academic 'whipping-boy' for Anne Boleyn scholars. She has written a biography that depicts Anne as a witch who suffered a miscarriage that produced a monstrous foetus recognised as the work of the devil. It is an interpretation offered with only a single hard fact to support the thesis: the report of the Marquis and Marchioness of Exeter's statement, as recorded by the unreliable imperial ambassador, that Henry had said in absolute secrecy that his marriage had been 'seduced and constrained by sortileges', in other words witchcraft. All the rest is thoughtful surmise. This might rightly cause concern if her scholarly rivals were not equally vulnerable to the same criticism. Ives's theory that Anne was a victim of a political plot concocted by Thomas Cromwell essentially rests on a key statement by Eustace Chapuys that Cromwell had told him that he alone had 'put his mind to think up and plan' the coup against the queen. Bernard is in much the same boat, his argument that the queen's destruction was due to an inadvertent confession made by the Countess of Worcester to her brother being entirely based on a poem written by a minion in the French embassy. Clear, unbiased and incontrovertible evidence in the Anne Boleyn saga is as scarce as hen's teeth.

Lack of acceptable documentation does not worry Professor Warnicke, who approaches her thesis with enthusiasm and considerable acumen. Europe was indeed on the verge of a witchcraft pandemic, and Warnicke starts with the probably correct assumption that Henry, reflecting the mores of his century, believed in demons, witches and warlocks and that Anne was bewitching him. She summarises her theme by saying:

Information from a wide range of sources will be used to support the argument that she [Anne] miscarried a defective foetus in 1536. It was because Henry viewed this mishap as an evil omen, both for his lineage and his kingdom, that he had her accused of engaging in illicit sexual acts with five men and fostered rumours that she had afflicted him with impotence and had conspired to poison both his daughter Mary and illegitimate son, Henry, Duke of Richmond.[31]

Two of the five men accused of adultery with Anne are said to have violated the 1534 law making buggery a capital offence and a detestable 'Romishe unnatural act' and were regarded as devil worshippers. Whether they did in fact practice sodomy is left in studied vagueness, the goal being not the act itself but the legend that Anne and her male cohorts indulged in illicit sexual behaviour. Warnick seems to feel that the unanimous acceptance of their guilt by the trial jury was tantamount to having committed illicit sex acts. The queen's demonic behaviour is further proven by the accusation of having bewitched her male friends with gifts, caresses and French kisses. The story of a monstrous foetus is regarded as the key to the efforts to demonise the queen and to Henry's frantic efforts to deny parentage.

The existence of an effective conservative faction at court bent on achieving a specific agenda that included destroying Anne is denied, and Cromwell's role in the plot is turned into a purely administrative performance doing the king's bidding. 'It was not a coalition of factions that brought down Anne but Henry's disaffection caused by her miscarriage of a defective child, the one act, beside adultery, that would certainly destroy his trust in her. Someone was to blame for God's visitation of that tragedy upon his nursery, and Henry would never admit to any culpability.'[32]

Cromwell was busy feeding Chapuys the misinformation that the king's continued friendship with France was due entirely to Anne's ability to influence the king, and that this was the reason why Cromwell wanted to be rid of her. Though Lancelot de Carles is mentioned as a source for Anne's seven years in France as an adolescent, he is dismissed as a creditable observer of the queen's downfall because he reverses the order of Anne's and her brother's trial. She does, however, introduce the Countess of Worcester, who is central to Carles's story, as a key government witness against the queen. Warnicke refuses to accept the hypothesis that the five men charged were all selected by Cromwell as members of the rival Boleyn party at court and argues he picked them because they all had reputations for 'lecherous habits', fitting nicely into Anne's own alleged promiscuity. Warnicke is willing, however, to accept Weston as a sodomite on the grounds that he asked forgiveness for acts of 'abominations' in his scaffold speech. She firmly believes that 'Henry genuinely believed that Anne was guilty of the crimes for which she died'[33] and twice quotes Thomas Cranmer's words to his king as an insightful conclusion to her troubled life:

For I never had better opinion in woman, than I had in her; which maketh me to think, that she should not be culpable. And again, I think your Highness would not have gone so far, except she had surely been culpable. Now I think that your Grace best knoweth, that next unto Your Grace, I was most bound unto her of all creatures living.[34]

What is most disturbing about Warnicke's work is not its lack of evidence supporting the existence of a defective foetus but the portrayal of the king who appears as a two-dimensional paper portrait whose purpose is more decorative than functional. To fit the role assigned him he should appear as a strong, single-minded sovereign bent on doing what he regards as being right. As Warnicke paints him, however, he is a flat, characterless figure. In most of the biographies of Anne Boleyn her husband does not fare well not because, as in Ives's case, he is depicted as a weak, easily manipulated monarch or in the case of Bernard, where he is regarded as a strong king, but because no details or proof of his character are supplied by the authors. Henry is just assumed to be whatever they want him to be to fit their interpretation of Anne's life.

Alison Weir
The Lady in the Tower: The Fall of Anne Boleyn

Alison Weir is the apple in the midst of the oranges, producing a 411-page coverage of the final three and a half months of Anne's career compared to the handling of her entire life by her colleague biographers. The consequences are obvious; far more and richer detail, many more and fuller quotations compared to short snippets and passing mention, and a far greater sense of verisimilitude and reality. All of these benefits make up for failing to tell the reader anything really new; Weir reiterates Ives's thesis that Cromwell was the mastermind of a political plot to destroy the queen with Henry playing a passive and minor role. On the other hand, what we lose on the curves we make up on the straightaway: Alison Weir offers the reader *haute cuisine* literary fare compared to the adequate academic meat and potatoes of her rivals.

Weir starts, as do many of her biographical colleagues, with dire warnings about Eustace Chapuys, acknowledging that he was a distinguished ecclesiastical judge, canon lawyer, and humanist but pointing out that his dispatches to Emperor Charles V were hopelessly prejudiced, that Anne was his 'bête noire', and scarcely a thing he says can be believed. Quoting William Paget, the king's Principal Secretary later in the reign, Weir describes Chapuys as a 'great practicer, tale-telling, lying and flattering' man who spoke 'without respect of honesty or truth, so it might serve his turn'[35] but then, like her three associates, she ignores her own excellent advice and relies heavily on Chapuys's reports in the *Calendar of State Papers, Spanish* to tell her story and prove her solution to the Anne Boleyn conundrum. The Anne depicted is not the fresh twenty-year-old who appeared at the English court in 1521 but an experienced, middle-aged (by sixteenth-century standards) queen of thirty-six who has begun to lose her looks, a 'thin old lady' who had become increasingly 'haughty, overbearing, shrewish and volatile, qualities that were frowned upon in wives, who were expected to be meek and submissive'.[36]

35. Anne Boleyn in later life having become distinctly jowly.

During the brief three years of their married life the king's blind passion had begun to wane, there was 'much coldness and grumbling' and there were increasingly moments when 'the Lady wants something, there is no one who dares contradict her, not even the king himself, because when he does not want to do what she wishes, she behaves like someone in a frenzy'.[37] These words, of course, come from Chapuys, and who can say whether to believe them or not. Weir follows Ives in presenting the queen as 'a passionate and sincere evangelical', the possessor of 'a library of radical reformist literature', and someone 'sympathetic to radical and even Lutheran ideas'; a description stronger than any found in Ives but of little importance to Weir's story since the queen's religious beliefs are not central to the last months of her life.

Weir commences in detail her saga of Anne's final days with the queen's miscarriage; on the morning of 29 January 1536 she aborted 'with much peril of her life a still-born foetus that had the appearance of a male child of fifteen weeks growth'. Five days before her miscarriage, Henry, while jousting at Greenwich 'fell so heavily' from his steed 'that everyone thought it was a miracle he was not killed' and feared him dead for two hours. It was said that word of the king's near-fatal accident so frightened the queen that she 'took such a fright withal that it caused her to fall in travail, and so was delivered afore her full time'. Anne became 'a woman full of sorrow', and the king was devastated at the loss of yet another son. Henry curtly told her 'clearly God did not wish to give him male children'. This led to a row in which Anne shouted 'he had no one to blame for this latest disappointment which had been caused by her distress of mind' about his fall from his horse and her anger over his blatant interest in 'that wench Seymour'. Henry then left the room 'with much ill grace' announcing he would speak to her after she had recovered from her miscarriage.[38] The queen's position was further weakened by the death of Katherine of Aragon. The king was now a liberated man, making Anne's position even more vulnerable than ever, for Anne was now older than Katherine had been when she conceived her last stillborn infant.

Royal marital relations deteriorated slowly to the point that Henry in anger claimed he had been seduced into marriage by sorcery and witchcraft and was seriously thinking of ending his marriage. If he did, it would mean starting afresh with no one harping about an illegal union and illegitimate children. Moreover, it was plain to the king that God in denying him a male offspring was not pleased with his current marriage. As tension between the royal couple increased, matters were made worse by the knowledge that Anne was thoroughly disliked both as a woman and as a queen by most of the king's subjects. They resented the 'goggle-eyed whore' claiming the title of Queen of England, and they asked 'Who the devil made Anne Bullen, that whore, queen?' Londoners called her a 'common stewed whore' and thought she should be burned at the stake. It was reported in France that 'the lower people are so violent against the Queen that they say a thousand ill and improper things against her'.[39] She received most of the blame for the execution in 1535 of Sir Thomas More, Bishop John Fisher and the Carthusian monks, all of whom had died refusing to take the oath of loyalty acknowledging the validity of her marriage and the legitimacy of her daughter Elizabeth.

At this point Weir introduces Thomas Cromwell, the king's Principal Secretary. Chapuys thought him 'a person of good cheer, gracious in words and generous in actions'.

Cardinal Wolsey was less complimentary and found him 'ready at all things, evil and good' while his usher, George Cavendish, thought him excelling all others in 'extorting power and insatiate tyranny'. Henry VIII beat him over the head and thought him socially unfit to lead his government but found him indispensable. Weir accepts him as a Machiavellian and something of 'a ruffian' and like Ives is strangely tolerant of the man who lined the path to political power with the corpses of the five men accused of having committed adultery with the queen. She does not, however, subscribe to the theory that Cromwell was ever joined to the queen in political or religious tandem. They operated separately.

Not only did Anne and Cromwell operate independently, in February they had a first-class row in which Anne accused Cromwell of corruption. Under the guise of reforming the monasteries, he and others, she claimed, were in fact destroying them to get at their riches to line their own pockets, and she threatened to inform the king. To make matters more difficult for Anne, rumours were spreading that the king was planning to rid himself of his wife and marry Jane Seymour. The imperial ambassador caustically commented that the king might indeed marry the 'well-tutored' Jane but that he would marry her only on condition she is a maid, 'and when he wants a divorce, there will be plenty of witnesses ready to testify that she was not'.[40]

By April, Cromwell had decided that Anne was too great a threat to him and had to go; the Skip lecture accusing the king's council of seizing Church property and wealth for their own profit was a gauntlet thrown in Cromwell's face. On April the Principal Secretary told Chapuys that an annulment of the marriage, which was all the king wanted, was not enough; the queen had to be physically eliminated. 'The evidence,' Weir writes, 'therefore strongly suggests that it was Cromwell, rather than Henry VIII, who was the prime mover in the matter.'[41] It is a myth that the king, disgusted with Anne, deprived of a male heir and in love with Jane Seymour, ordered Cromwell to find and implement the most efficient way of ridding himself of his unpleasant and unproductive spouse. As Weir puts it, it is recognised today that what has been called 'the most rapid and bloody political crisis of the century' originated with the king's Principal Secretary 'who had good cause to believe that Anne's influence with the king posed a threat to his policies and to his very life'. Ms Weir concludes by joining the chorus that 'Henry was suggestible', always an essential ingredient in explaining the 'truth' of the political solution to what happened.[42]

At this point our author announces a partial retreat from the Ives thesis, acknowledging that it is unknown whether Cromwell manufactured the entire scenario from scratch or merely took advantage of accidental evidence that happened to fall into his lap. She accepts the sincerity of the secretary's statement a month after the plot had been hatched and the trap sprung that he had 'thought up and plotted' the entire affair but she asks the critical question, 'What prompted the idea of accusing Anne of sexual crimes?' As we shall see, that is a crucial question. The answer lies in Lancelot de Carles's story of Elizabeth, Countess of Worcester's confession to her brother as to what was going on in the queen's chambers. Weir limits, however, de Carles's information to the suggestion of improper behaviour in the queen's household and the statement that Mark Smeton could tell a great deal more. There are two versions as to who told the king of his wife's alleged adulteries with Smeton and others. There is de Carles's picture of Anthony Browne and two other men informing Henry, who calmly accepted the news and ordered a full investigation, and that of Alexander Aless, the Scottish Lutheran and friend of Cromwell, who said the secretary and Thomas Wriothesley, the Lord Chancellor, told the king who 'was furious' but quickly 'dissembled his wrath' and ordered enquires.[43]

Henry receives a clean bill of morality; there is no evidence that he 'personally exerted himself to pervert the course of justice'. It was Cromwell's idea to charge Anne with sexual 'abomination' and infidelity. Henry was forced, Ives calls it 'bounced', into action when presented by Cromwell with a *fait accompli*. His decision had little or nothing to do with Jane Seymour or his obsession with a male heir to his throne.

Weir describes the five so-called adulterers in far greater detail than her colleagues. Viscount Rochford, Anne's brother, is pictured as an easy target to vilify. As the poet Thomas Wyatt put it, 'Hadst thou not been so proud, for thy wit, each man would thee bemoan'; possibly that wit was overly unkind and caustic. Sir Henry Norris was a great favourite of the king but also a staunch supporter of the Boleyn faction and regarded as a threat to the Principal Secretary. George Cavendish thought him overly ambitious and ungrateful to the monarch who had endowed him with power and wealth. Sir Francis Weston was a first-class athlete, a fine musician, and a proper match for his royal master. He was young, handsome, and of ancient birth and high accomplishment; George Cavendish, always critical of court favourites, thought that 'hot lust kindled the fire of filthy concupiscence' and had led him into the queen's bed. Sir William Brereton was well born and even better connected with extensive estates and crown offices in Wales. Since he was over fifty it is hard to paint him as a sexual Lothario but Cromwell detested him as a man who had deliberately murdered by legal means a man whom the Principal Secretary had personally deemed innocent. Cavendish thought him a victim of 'old rancor'. Finally there was that varlet Mark Smeton, a handsome young Flemish devil, a lutenist and keyboard player with a divine voice; Cavendish called him 'a singing boy'. Success had gone to his head and he was 'very grand' and overbearing in his insolence to others. When Cromwell got hold of him he broke very easily and probably no torture had to be used. He alone actually confessed to sexual intercourse with the queen.[44]

What these men all had in common was their close proximity to Anne's chambers and potential for misconduct, and their alleged licentiousness. Cromwell was interested in their shock value on the king and presumably five cases therefore were better than one, although the secretary might well have preferred the higher number because of his training in copiousness where five examples were always regarded as being more effective than one. Equal to Mark Smeton's confession in shock value was the accusation that Rochford had committed incest with his sister. Part of the evidence for this came from the Countess of Worcester's account that George had appeared one evening in the queen's bedchamber dressed only in his bedclothes. The fatal evidence, however, was supplied by Lord Rochford's wife who, allegedly without solicitation, went to Cromwell and told him that not only had her husband had sex with Anne but also that the two had laughed in bed and discussed the king's erectile dysfunction and general ineptitude as a lover.

Why Anne's sister-in-law said all this has never been adequately explained by any biographer, but many motives have been offered. She was jealous of her husband's close association with Anne; she was furious with Anne for an alleged scandal at court that had led to her dismissal from her position close to the royal sun; she was outraged at George for being a homosexual and sleeping with Mark Smeton (this is suggested by Retha Warnicke); she was a secret supporter of Katherine of Aragon and her daughter Mary and acted in revenge against Anne. Alison Weir says that possibly she realised that the Boleyns were on their way out and since she was married to a particularly vulnerable Boleyn she was in great danger unless she proved otherwise. Whatever her reasons, her evidence clinched the plot against the queen and possibly more than anything else proved fatal to her husband. Anne had betrayed and humiliated her royal husband as a man and as a king, turning, as George Cavendish said, 'trust [in]to treason' and Henry's 'lust [in]to hatred'. Little wonder Alexander Aless describes a final meeting of the royal family with Elizabeth in the queen's arms, displaying that the king was deeply angered, 'although he could conceal his anger wonderfully well'.[45]

So far the crown's case against Anne was limited to sex; later their sins would encompass regicide. Clear evidence would have to wait still Anne was imprisoned in the Tower. Placed in fairly luxurious confinement but surrounded by friendless agents of the government, Anne made the fatal mistake of talking too much. She narrated her conversation with Norris and spoke of dead men's shoes and marrying once the king was dead, which in Cromwell's adroit hands became a clear case of anticipating, even planning the king's death. Even Archbishop Cranmer was shocked into acceptance of the queen's treason by the addition of regicide, and wrote his sovereign that he was 'exceedingly sorry that such faults can be proved by the Queen ... but I am, and ever shall be, your faithful subject'.[46]

Of all the victims Sir Richard Page and Sir Thomas Wyatt are the most unusual for, although arrested as Boleynites and potential paramours of the queen, they escaped the fatal consequences of treason and were released. A good deal is known or more accurately 'said' about Sir Thomas. He was vigorously defended by his grandson George Wyatt, and the *Spanish Chronicle*, edited by H. A. S. Hume, has much to say (possibly entirely apocryphal) about the poet's relations with both Anne and Henry. The *Spanish Chronicle* states that Wyatt informed the king that he had first-hand knowledge his future queen was unchaste but Henry refused to believe him, dismissing Wyatt's assertion that Anne was 'not meet to be coupled with Your Grace'. 'Her conversation,' the poet maintained, 'hath been so loose and base, which thing I know not so much by hearsay as by my own experience, as one that have had my carnal pleasure with her.' Henry is said to have been 'somewhat astounded' by the news but oddly thanked Wyatt for his honesty and tells him 'to make no more words of this matter to any man living'. Most readers have rightly wondered why Wyatt ever lived to tell this tale. Instead of ordering Wyatt's death, he made him chief ewerer at Anne's Coronation and in 1535 promoted him to the Privy Council. The story became even more fantastic when the *Spanish Chronicle* reported that Wyatt while in the Tower penned a letter to the king detailing his relations with Anne and stating that Henry had told Wyatt that he wished to marry Anne; 'what do you think about it?' The poet informed him that she was a 'bad woman'. The king in great wrath immediately banished him from court refusing to hear his reasons. In his letter from the Tower Wyatt now states his reasons: he visited Anne one evening in her chamber whilst she was in bed. He confesses his undying love and asks to receive consolation for his tortured heart. He kisses her, touches her, 'took liberties lower down', and began to take his clothes off. A great stumping noise was heard overhead, Anne got up and left the room to investigate and more than a hour later returned without an ounce of passion left in her. Wyatt drew his own conclusions, and admitted that a week later he 'had my way with her'. He concludes, 'If your Majesty, when you banished me, had permitted me to speak, I should have told you what I now write.'[47]

On 6 May, according to Weir, another letter was penned, this time by Anne. Most specialists deem it to be historical fiction, an extremely well-written forgery described by one expert as 'one of the finest compositions in the English language'. It is headed 'To the King from the Lady in the Tower', the title of Alison Weir's biography. It is a model of exquisitely polite defiance: You ask me to confess the truth,

I shall with all willingness and duty perform your command. But let not your Grace imagine that your poor wife will ever be brought to acknowledge a fault where not so much as a thought ever proceeded. And to speak a truth, never a prince had wife more loyal in all duty and all true affection, than you have ever found in Anne Bulen [*sic*].

She thanks her sovereign for having 'chosen her from low estate to be your queen' and asks for a lawful trial to either clear her innocence and end the 'ignominy and slander of the world' or reveal her 'guilt openly declared'. She then twists the knife:

If you have already determined of me, and that not only my death but an infamous slander must bring you the joying of your desired happiness, then I desire of God that He pardon your great sin herein...

She concludes by asking 'that myself only may bear the burden of your Grace's displeasure, and that it may not touch the innocent souls of those poor gentlemen who, as I understand are likewise in strait imprisonment for my sake'.[48] Ms Weir wants very badly for this letter to be authentic and cites Jasper Ridley as a modern historian who believes it is. Since Ridley wrote a biography of Henry VIII comparing the king to Hitler and Stalin, sceptics may question his judgement. Certainly Anne's final letter shows no similarity to Anne's epistle to Cardinal Wolsey quoted previously (see page 96).

From the early seventeenth century when the royal supremacy was first seriously questioned and the tyranny of the nation state came under attack, Anne Boleyn's biographers have struggled with her trial for treason, invariably comparing both the process and the decision to modern concepts of justice. We are told that the accused heard the charges for the first time only when they were brought into court. They had to defend themselves without benefit of council, could call no witness on their behalf and there was no cross-examination of government witnesses. Weir assumes the system was hopelessly rigged against the accused and that Anne was framed. She quotes Cardinal Wolsey's estimation of sixteenth-century justice: 'If the Crown were prosecutor and asserted it, justice would be found to bring a verdict that Abel was the murderer of Cain.'[49]

There were two sets of trials, for commoners – Smeton, Norris, Weston and Brereton – and those of noble status – the queen and her brother George, Lord Rochford. The charge for those of lesser rank was that they had 'violated and had carnal knowledge of the Queen' and had conspired the king's death with Anne. The jury unanimously pronounced all four men guilty of fornication with the queen and conspiring the death of the king. Anne and her brother were tried three days later in the 80 by 50-foot King's Hall in the Tower of London. A raised dais had been constructed in the centre of the hall to display the accused, the jury of twenty-six peers, the Duke of Norfolk as Lord High Steward sitting under a special canopy bearing the king's arms, and the Duke of Suffolk seated on his left. At the duke's right sat the Lord Chancellor, a commoner without a vote but present to give advice on legal matters, and at his feet sat Norfolk's nineteen-year-old son, the Earl of Surrey, carrying the golden staff of his father's office as Earl Marshal of the realm. The great hall was lined with benches to seat the expected crowd of sightseers – possibly 2,000. The men sitting in judgement represented a large percentage of the peerage, whether they had been selected for their known dislike of the queen or their willingness to do the king's bidding is not clear. Lord Dacre only the year before had been acquitted in his trial for high treason. One senses that this time the government was going to be more sure of the verdict. Weir, unlike the other authors, says that very likely Anne's father, the Earl of Wiltshire, was a member of his daughter's jury.

The crown made the most of the queen's conversation with Norris and the intimation that she planned to marry as soon as the king was dead. She was accused of having kissed her brother and of informing him that she was pregnant, thereby suggesting that he might be the father. Worse, they were charged with having laughed together at the king's dress and his poetry, which was described as 'a great crime' because it proved she did not love him and was tired of him.⁵⁰ The guilty verdict was delivered individually by each member of the jury, those of the lowest hereditary rank first. Her uncle the Duke of Norfolk spoke the final judgement: 'Thou shalt be burnt here within the Tower of London on the green, else to have thy head smitten off, as the king's pleasure shall be further known of the same.'

Anne said only the bare minimum throughout the trial, her face unchanging when she heard the death sentence. Then in the words given her by Crispin de Milherve, a bystander, she spoke to the assembled crowd watching her trial:

My lords, I will not say your sentence is unjust, nor presume that my reasons can prevail against your convictions. I am willing to believe that you have sufficient reasons for what you have done but then they must be other than those which have been produced in court, for I am clear of all the offences which you then laid to my charge. I have ever been a faithful wife to the King, though I do not say I have always shown him that humility which his goodness to me, and the honours to which he raised me, merited ... Think not I say this in the hope to prolong my life, for He who saveth from death hath taught me how to die, and He will strengthen my faith ... As for my brother and those others who are unjustly condemned, I would willingly suffer many deaths to deliver them, but since I see it so pleases the King, I shall willingly accompany them in death, with this assurance, that I shall lead an endless life with them in peace and joy, where I will pray to God for the King and for you, my lords.[51]

George, Lord Rochford's trial did not go as smoothly as his sister's, and he was a great deal more vocal. When handed a paper purporting to prove that Anne had told his wife that the king 'has not the ability to copulate with a woman for he had neither potency nor vigour', he promptly read 'in great contempt of Cromwell' the entire paper aloud to the enthralled audience, saying that he did not want to 'arouse suspicion which might prejudice the king's issue', which, of course, he had.[52] He responded to the other charges against him so convincingly that the bookie betting was ten to one that he would be acquitted. Lancelot de Carles thought 'his calm behaviour and good defence' was equal to Sir Thomas More's spectacular performance at his trial, but also like Sir Thomas he was unanimously found guilty. Norfolk read the grisly sentence: his body to be hanged by the neck, mutilated while still living, and the bits and pieces distributed throughout the kingdom wherever 'the king should assign'. According to the imperial ambassador, Rochford announced that 'since he must die, he would no longer maintain his innocence, but confessed that he had deserved death'.[53] Mercifully a traitor's death was not performed on Rochford or on the other victims.

Weir's considered conclusion is that without exception all the verdicts were politically motivated, with nothing to do with justice, and the vultures immediately gathered to pick over the bodies. Rochford was said to be worth £441 (in modern money £154,200), Brereton £1,236 (£431,850), Norris £1,327 (£463,700), not to mention their offices and pensions. Young Francis Weston, though he came from a wealthy family, was far too heavily in debt to be of any interest to the fortune seekers; he owed money to the king, his father, his father's cook, his cousin, his draper, one of the pages of the Privy Council, the king's goldsmith, his tailor, his shoemaker and his barber, in sum a handsome total of £925 (£323,150).[54]

A French swordsman, hired days before the execution to give him time to arrive, was reserved for Anne. Since there is no record of the queen asking for the French sword we do not know why Henry bothered except perhaps because the sword was regarded as being more accurate than the axe. An English axe was used on the others, probably including Smeton, whom George Cavendish thought worthy of a full traitor's death replete with partial hanging and castration. Since there are multiple versions of what each victim said while awaiting execution, historical fiction entered their lives even before they had left it. According to George Constantine, who watched all but the queen die and 'heard them and wrote every word they spake', every one of them 'in a manner' confessed although not necessarily to the crime for which they were condemned, and all admitted that they deserved to die for having led sinful lives.[55] Rochford as the highest rank met the axe first, then followed Norris, Weston and Brereton. Poor lowly Smeton went last, the headless corpses pushed aside to make room and the block awash with blood.

Next day, 19 May, was Anne Boleyn's turn. She had been informed at 7 a.m., the execution scheduled for 9 a.m. The procession that left the queen's lodging for the scaffold located in the courtyard between the Jewel House and King's Hall included 200 Yeomen of the Guard, the officers of the Tower, Constable of the Tower Sir William Kingston, and finally Anne, escorted by four ladies and probably her Almoner John Skip. The executioner, dressed in black with his upper face masked, along with his assistant, waited on the scaffold. The Earl of Wiltshire was not present to watch his daughter die but both Dukes of Norfolk and Suffolk were present along with possibly 1,000 spectators.

There are many variants of Anne's final words but they are very different from those delivered at the end of her trial; this time there were neither avowals of innocence or defiance, only the accepted formula for dying well.

Good friends, I am not come here to excuse or to justify myself, forasmuch as I know full well that aught that I could say in my defence doth not appertain to you, and that I could draw no hope of life from the same. But I come only to die, and thus to yield myself humbly to the will of the King, my lord. And if in my life I did ever offend the King's Grace, surely with my death I do now atone for the same. And I blame not my judges, nor any other manner of person, nor anything save the cruel law of the land by which I die. But be this, and my faults, as they may, I beseech you all, good friends, to pray for the life of the King, my sovereign lord and yours who is one of the best princes on the face of the Earth, and who hath always treated me so well that better could not be; wherefore I submit to death with a good will, humbly asking pardon of all the world.[56]

The executioner begged her pardon, received it and asked her to kneel and say her prayers. While she was doing so his blade flashed, and, as Judge Sir John Spelman put it, 'He did his office before you could say a paternoster.' There is no record that the head was held aloft; it simply fell to the floor and Spelman observed 'her lips moving and her eyes moving'. Sir Thomas Wyatt turned her death into poetry:

So freely wooed, so dearly bought,
So soon a queen, so soon low brought
Hath not been seen, could not be thought.
O! What is Fortune?[57]

36. An imaginative and romantic depiction of Anne on the execution
scaffold preparing for death. Authenticity requires that the executioner
be masked and the sword hidden from sight under a mound of straw.

8

The King's Mind

Without exception all four of the biographers under review have endured spells of envy of the historical novelist for the excellent reason that fiction writers are not chained to historical facts and are free to assign imaginary motives and invent dramatic events at will. In fact they are complimented when they do so, while the biographer-historian is condemned for ignoring or misinterpreting documents. When dealing with the likes of Anne Boleyn, whose life and character has been battered and doctored by both a paucity of documents and a legion of religious and personal biases, the historian does out of desperation what the fiction writer does by choice: indulge in make-believe.

All four of our authors engage in extensive fantasy that historians dignify by describing as speculation and surmise. Warnicke, the most aggressive, has Anne's deformed and monstrous foetus for which there is not a scrape of sound proof and considerable, if weak, evidence for denying as a perfectly normal male child. Bernard has his epic poem by Lancelot de Carles that he argues is a legitimate account by a well-placed observer who must be believed, not a fanciful tale penned by a minion in the French embassy without any reliable information except his imagination.

The insurmountable weakness of Ives's and Weir's theory that Thomas Cromwell manufactured a plot to destroy the queen is that it does not fit the known facts, of which there are deplorably few, or the characters of the Principal Secretary and the king. It is beyond belief that an intelligent, ingenious and experienced high government official would build a battleship to do the work of a row-boat. It is heinous to turn the secretary into an ogre who remorselessly contrived the death of five men simply because they were available and it was politically convenient to do so. There was neither the time nor the need for such an intricate plot, requiring five men to be accused and found guilty of adultery, when a simpler and far easier crime to fabricate and prove, such as theft or embezzlement by a single person, would have sufficed. Ives and Weir have to postulate the need for a major scandal aimed at Henry's most sensitive characteristic – his pride and sense of honour – to shock him out of his dependence on and faith in his Boleyn marriage. As Bernard says, the whole elaborate and time-consuming affair lacks 'proportions'.[1] The entire scheme had to be arranged in a matter of days, the victims found, interrogated and their crimes proven in sufficient fashion to convince the king and 'bounce' him into action. Anyone familiar with the tortoise-like quality of most governmental enterprises would question the existence of a plot on the basis of the time available alone.

One of the least satisfactory aspects of the Cromwellian thesis is the choice of victims. It is presumed they were selected for political reasons although any clear evidence is desperately scarce. It is maintained that the Principal Secretary's purpose was not only to destroy the queen but also her political faction but not a single member of the group fits comfortably the description of a political enemy. No history of animosity between Anne's brother George, Lord Rochford, and Cromwell is offered except the presumption that he, like his sister, was pro-French and anti-imperial. It seems unlikely that Cromwell would have arranged the political murder of a man who was close to him religiously, both men being religious reformers, advocates of the Bible in English and anti-clerical. It is impossible to categorise the Principal Secretary's religious beliefs with precision but shortly after George's execution Cromwell achieved Lord Rochford's passionate goal of an English Bible in every church. Both men were accused of being Lutherans, and Cromwell was branded at his death in 1540 as a heretical sacramentarian. The only firm evidence we have of his faith is his statement to the Lutheran envoys negotiating an alliance between England and the Lutheran princes of Germany that, though he favoured their religious position, 'as the world now stood he would believe even as his master, the king, believed'.[2]

The evidence of enmity on the part of Norris, Weston, Brereton and Smeton is even weaker. Norris was a political heavyweight in the king's Privy Chamber but no proof is offered that he was a Cromwellian rival. Weston's name is on the list not because he was a rival but because he wasn't: he was, it is said, selected to conceal the fact that Cromwell was manufacturing a political coup and his value to Cromwell was that he had no political affiliations and therefore people would be misled as to the real purpose of the plot, which was political; his very innocence caused his death by a bloody-minded and absolutely ruthless fellow servant of the crown. Ives can find no reason at all for the selection of Sir William Brereton except to surmise some long ago but not forgotten altercation with Cromwell. No one can imagine Mark Smeton the musician as being a danger to the king's chief minister, and if Cromwell discovered him it must have been the ill will and jealousy he generated by his lavish living beyond his means and station in life that alerted him as a candidate to be carefully interrogated. The political rivalry theory simply does not hold together, and their assumed second common denominator – they were all oversexed, licentious individuals who would be attractive to a wanton queen – is little more than the murmur of court gossip filtered though the lecherous mind of George Cavendish.

The only way that Cromwell could have fabricated his story of adultery in the queen's chamber in time to trigger the plot was to get his information from another source, and that leads to Bernard's insistence that Lancelot de Carles's verses must be believed. It makes the best sense of any of the proposed explanations for Anne's disgrace and destruction because it not only explains how the king was informed but also accounts for the individuals involved: they were all members of a cadre of men who had entrée into the queen's privy chambers. There were seven of them, the five executed for adultery and treason plus Richard Page and Thomas Wyatt, who were later exonerated and liberated from the Tower. The story of the accidental conversation between Sir Anthony Browne and his sister Elizabeth, Countess of Worcester as narrated by Professor Bernard has already been told: what he calls the unlucky and quite accidental revelation by the countess of the hanky-panky in the queen's bedchamber which was offered as justification for her own extra-martial pregnancy. What started as dangerous court gossip became scandal tainted with treason that could not be kept from the king, and Sir Anthony, supported by two friends, felt obligated to inform Henry, who handled it as he treated all dangerous rumours: he ordered, presumably Cromwell, to investigate and reveal the truth. The Principal Secretary commenced the investigation with the most vulnerable and least respectable member of the group, Mark Smeton, the king's prize musician and singer and the queen's preferred virginal player, who did not possess the social status to prevent the use of torture, if it was required, to help along the interrogation. Smeton confessed to three sexual encounters with Anne; Cromwell and Thomas Wriothesley promptly reported to the king confirming the truth of the Countess of Worcester's words. Henry was deeply shocked, and all seven culprits plus the queen were imprisoned in the Tower of London for further questioning, Smeton being transferred from Cromwell's house to the Tower.

What had happened was that a rumour based on court gossip and confirmed by a questionable confession extracted from a mere varlet became not only a lucky break for Cromwell, offering him the means to 'bounce' the king's thinking about his wife, but it also disclosed what the king, the court and the entire realm accepted as the hand of god revealed to mortal men. As we discussed in chapter 3, the sixteenth century viewed luck, chance, fortune and coincidence as figments of the human imagination proceeding 'first of ignorance and want of true knowledge, not considering what God is, and by whose only foresight and providence, all things in the world are seen of Him before they come to pass'. In a teleological universe in which an all-seeing and interfering god resided, a lucky happenstance such as the countess's disclosure could not be accidental but had to possess moral meaning. God was informing the king and all England of the truth about Anne Boleyn. Certainly this was Archbishop Cranmer's reaction when he wrote Henry VIII, 'God hath sent her this punishment, for that she feignedly hath professed his gospel in her mouth, and not in her heart and deed.'³ For a king already tired of a nagging and outspoken spouse, desperately asking God for a male heir from a wife who seemed to be incapable of giving birth to the male of the species, and constantly seeking outside blame for all the trials and tribulations that beset him as a man and as a king, the explosive news of Anne's alleged adultery was both a curse and a blessing. It shamed the king as a cuckolded husband but it liberated him to try a third wife and gain a male heir. It also explains the intensity of Henry's reactions to the news of Anne's betrayal: God himself had uncovered her sins. The Weston family's offer of a huge bribe to purchase a pardon for young Sir Francis was not allowed to deflect the king's sense of divine justice and need to punish everyone involved in the queen's sinfulness; not even Sir Henry Norris, Henry's closest friend, was spared.

April 1536 was not the first time Henry had been spoken to by the voice of God. Eleven years earlier he had either read or been informed of Levicitus's promise of death to the children of the man who dared, even unknowingly, marry the his deceased brother's wife. Henry's conscience immediately burst into an all-consuming flame that insisted on the annulment of his marriage, even at the risk of his soul's entrance into heaven. Not even Katherine's sworn oath that she had come to his bed a virgin could convince him she was not lying; God had told him otherwise. Now God had spoken again, and the king's reactions were almost identical: conscience and conviction exploded for a second time, and almost every biographer of the queen has commented on the intensity of her husband's conviction that she was guilty of multiple adultery. As Alison Weir, quoting David Loades, a respected author and Tudor expert, puts it, 'the suddenness or the vehemence of Henry's reaction' requires a cataclysmic event, that was the countess's accidental revelation, which was immediately translated into the voice of God.

Professor Ives's and Alison Weir's Cromwellian solution presupposes not only Anne's innocence, which is a major attraction, but it also demands an imaginary and malleable Henry VIII who was 'highly persuadable', what Weir calls 'suggestibility'. Such a man, however, is quite contrary to historical reality. To allow Anne and Cromwell freedom to perform their assigned roles of strong-minded, charismatic femme fatale and scheming, ruthless government official, Henry must be turned into an easily moulded and highly impressionable weakling. That is a Henry who is hard to find. Both Ives and Weir are categorical in their conviction that Cromwell was acting on his own, that the king in no way instigated the destruction of his queen and left the entire affair to his ministers once the Principal Secretary's fallacious claims about Anne's actions were brought to his attention. Alison Weir puts it as follows: 'The evidence therefore strongly suggests that it was Cromwell, rather than Henry VIII, who was the prime mover in the matter,' and 'there is absolutely nothing to support the theory that Henry VIII passed on to Cromwell the task of finding the quickest and most effective way of getting rid of her.'[4] Ives's wording is more dramatic: 'When, late in Easter Week 1536, Cromwell put his mind, as he said, to "think up and plan" the coup against Anne, he faced the biggest challenge of his life.'[5] The truth of the matter is that there is absolutely no acceptable evidence one way or the other. To state that the king was a mere observer in what happened or that he was the chief instigator and perpetrator is pure speculation, what fiction writers call make-believe.

37. The famous Holbein cartoon study for the mural of Henry VIII displayed in Whitehall Palace, which was destroyed when the building burned in January 1698, is the image of the king best remembered by history. It is scarcely the picture of a sovereign easily manipulated, duped or influenced.

This being the case, can we at least say that a certain line of action fits the character of the king or Cromwell? We have already discussed the king's chief minister but what about Henry? Here the known and documented personality and mental habits of Henry VIII, as opposed to the stated character as pronounced by his biographers, become all-important. If there is one thing Henry learned as king for thirty-eight years it was suspicion of his ministers; he was constantly on the lookout for self-interest, deliberate misinformation, and temporising 'for their own profit'. As early as June 1516, when he was only twenty-five, Henry announced to the Venetian ambassador, 'I don't choose that any one shall have it in his power to command me.'[6] Twenty years later he would never have allowed the low-born servant, Thomas Cromwell, the son of a blacksmith who dealt in cloth and owned a brewery, to manipulate him with false information about his wife whom he still respected if not loved.

Both Stephen Gardiner, Bishop of Winchester, and Secretary William Paget warned of the consequence of being caught out trying to influence the king. Paget said that the wily bishop was 'too wise to take upon himself to govern the King' or 'enter any dangerous matters, not knowing certain, by himself, whether His Grace would allow them or not'.[7] When Sir Thomas Seymour during the final years of the reign tried to turn Henry against Archbishop Cranmer, the king immediately guessed his purpose – Seymour was fronting for a group of land speculators bent on plundering clerical lands – and publicly humiliated the inexperienced man in such a way as to expose him as a damn fool.[8] It was mandatory that a minister know the workings of the king's mind, and when Bishop Stokesley, Bishop of London, in early 1536 was asked if he knew whether the king would 'abandon' his wife and seek an annulment of his marriage, he answered, 'He would not give any opinion to anyone but the King himself, and before doing so he would know the King's own inclination.'[9]

What Henry wanted most was meticulous and accurate information from his ministers, and in a letter to Bishop Tunstal, his envoy in Paris, he outlined his expectations: it was the king's duty to 'God and the world' to 'search, examine and inquire where should rest the culpe, blame, default and occasion of so many evils, to the intent that, the cause once removed and extirpated, the effects of the same may also be disappointed'.[10] Ralph Sadler once noted to Thomas Cromwell that 'as ye know his Grace is always loath to sign', not so much because he hated decision-making as because Henry was an inveterate nitpicker; he felt obliged to scrutinise every detail, study every authority, weight all the evidence and make up his mind slowly and thoroughly.[11] Having dotted every 'I' and crossed every 'T' to his ritualistic satisfaction he rarely changed his mind; as the imperial ambassador put it, 'When this king decides on anything he goes the whole length.' As a divine-right king who spoke to and for God, he could not go about changing his mind. Both Cardinal Campeggio and Ambassador Chapuys agreed, the cardinal exclaiming that once the king had made a decision 'if an angel was to descend from heaven, he would not be able to persuade him to the contrary' and the ambassador reporting that not all of the king's ministers combined could 'persuade him to follow a different course in politics unless the idea comes from him first'.[12] Erasmus put it another way: 'He attempted nothing which he did not bring to a successful conclusion.'[13] A sick and tired Cardinal Wolsey murmured on his deathbed, 'Be well advised and assured what ye put in his head, for ye shall never pull it out again.' Cromwell was more prosaic: 'It was a wonder to see how princely, with how excellent gravity and inestimable majesty His Majesty exercised the office of supreme head of his Church of England.'[14] In sum, not Ives's 'highly persuadable man'.

38. A lead medallion of Henry VIII, definitely not a man 'highly persuadable' nor would any of his subjects have accepted the vicar of Ticehurst's challenge to spit on its face.

Henry was never a reckless man; on the other hand he was an enthusiast, often emotionally overreacting and ignoring the consequence of his decisions. He refused to accept the betrayal of his fifth wife, Catherine Howard, until his council had gathered insurmountable evidence he could not ignore. He wept tears when he finally accepted the truth that his 'rose without a thorn' was not only sleeping about but had also been the common-law wife of another man before he met her, and he promised fearsome revenge. He also almost strangled the life out of his fool for calling his daughter Elizabeth a bastard. But even in a rage his majestic presence was awesome. John Hales wrote Sir Anthony Brown that in dealing with the king a subject had 'not to do with man but with a more excellent and divine estate' before which it was impossible to stand without trembling.[15] Thomas Wriothesley went further, warning that kings 'hath eyes and ears in the bottom of their bellies and the lining of their hearts' that could detect treason and fraudulence.[16] 'If God illuminated the eyes of the king' subjects disobeyed at their peril.[17] Cromwell summed up the difficulties and dangers of serving a man as complex and wily as Henry when he informed the imperial ambassador that 'princes were endowed with qualities of mind and peculiarities unknown to all other people' and that 'whoever trusts in the word of princes (who one day say one thing and on the next retract it) relies on them, or expects the fulfilment of their promises, is not a wise man'.[18] If the Principal Secretary really believed his own analysis of his sovereign, he would never have tried to misdirect him with false misinformation and a fictitious plot for Henry VIII was anything but Alison Weir's 'suggestible' king.

Henry was not a man unaware of the risks to his immortal soul that he was taking in his defiance of the pope and the Catholic world. 'Think you my lords,' he told his council at the height of the break with Rome, that apprehension – the fear that he might someday hang in hell – touches 'not my body and soul; think you that these doings do not daily and hourly trouble my conscience and vex my spirit?'[19] We have already encountered in an earlier chapter Henry, the man of tender conscience and ritualistic religious behaviour, and he was always ready to inspect and lecture other people on the purity of their lives and consciences, and to strike a blow for righteousness. He harangued his sister Margaret, Queen of Scotland, on the 'inevitable damnation' awaiting the adulteress. She had divorced her second husband on grounds far more questionable than Henry's divorce from Katherine of Aragon. And her brother warned 'what charge of conscience, what grudge and fretting yea, what danger of damnation' she brought upon her soul unless she 'as in conscience ye are bound under peril of God's everlasting indignation', forsook 'the adulterer's company with him that is not nor may not be of right your husband'.[20] Some may find this is the pot calling the kettle black, but, as in everything he did, Henry VIII was deadly serious.

39. Margaret Tudor, Henry VIII's sister who was married to James IV of Scotland and was the link to the Stuart line, had a married life almost as lurid as her brother's.

The picture presented above is neither of a man easily persuaded nor a king before whom Cromwell, a sensible man, would want to propose a plot based on lies, hearsay and falsification. Cromwell had been literally beaten about the head and back by his irate sovereign and he would not have wanted a repeat performance. Evidence, logic and characterisation certainly weaken the Cromwellian solution to Anne's destruction. This, however, does not necessarily clear the path for Lancelot de Carles; there is nothing to prove the validity of his story of the countess's indiscretions and its conveyance to the king. Moreover, his tale of misbehaviours in the queen's bedchamber makes

Anne out to be an adulteress, which many readers will find even more distasteful than viewing Cromwell as an infamous and bloody-minded monster. As with most things related to the Anne Boleyn yarn the evidence that the king knew about the queen's behaviour and betrayal from the start is scarce and uncertain. Certainly Anne herself did not blame Cromwell but named the king as having appointed Lady Boleyn and Mistress Coffin as attendants on the queen when she was in the Tower; 'the king wist what he did'. 'I think [it] much unkindness in the king to put about me as I never loved.'[21] Chapuys certainly suspected Henry's hand in what happened, and both the king and Archbishop Cranmer behaved as if God, not Cromwell, had spoken. The deity had opened the Countess of Worcester's mouth to speak words of truth that both men had to believe. As the archbishop wrote Henry, 'God hath sent her this punishment.'[22] Henry found no reason to argue with divine judgement; it fitted his needs and the mental and religious structure of his age. From this perspective Anne's trial was a forgone and heavenly conclusion.

Eric Ives's answer to all of this is to place one make-believe against another: he postulates that Lancelot de Carles's story of scandal in the queen's bedchamber fitted neatly the narrative Cromwell was in the process of fabricating because Cromwell had spread the tale of Anne's adulterous behaviour to the French ambassador, who then related it to de Carles. It was 'government issue' from the start; not a lucky accident. There is absolutely no evidence that the Principal Secretary informed the ambassador, nor is any reason offered why he should have done so. It is all hypothesis, no more or less substantive than claiming that de Carles had his own sources of information, which, as Professor Bernard maintains, should be believed.

The indisputable fact that twenty-seven lords of the kingdom, the best and most worthy portion of English society, voted without a single dissenting voice to pronounce the queen guilty of adultery, incest and treason has worried readers ever since God's direct interference in the affairs of mankind began to wane. The trial must have been rigged against her, the jury must have been threatened or corrupted, the evidence must have been faked, Mark Smeton's confession was the product of torture. Certainly the evidence as it has come down through the centuries is not convincing enough to convict the queen by modern standards of justice. Equally certain, we do not possess all the documentation though there is debate over how much is missing and why. All affidavits of the interrogations of Smeton, Norris and the queen have vanished; all we have are the written indictments accusing the queen and her five paramours, not the evidence presented by the government to prove its case although much of this may have been oral, not written. Cromwell as Master of the Rolls may well have censured the evidence; Elizabeth I may have ordered its destruction to suppress proof of her mother's guilt; mice and bookworms, enjoying cloth parchment, may have consumed the records. However, even with only partial documentation it is safe to say that Anne's jury had no choice but to find her guilty as charged. Not only did it recognise the hand of God at work but also by the logic of the doctrine of correspondence, the queen and her colleagues in sin were proven adulterers and traitors, conspiring the death of the king. The government did not have to prove an overt act, only the correspondence of her reputation to adulterous behaviour. Anne's evil words to Sir Henry Norris, 'you look for dead men's shoes; for if ought came to the king but good you would look to have me'; corresponded to adultery and treason because the evil thought was apparent. Both presiding judge and jury had been taught from childhood to 'search for the cause of every thing'; that might be the want of a horseshoe, a suppressed smile, or a lecherous reputation, all of which were just as valid evidence as an eyewitness to a treasonous or adulterous act.

All the government needed to do was to prove that Anne possessed the character of an adulterer and traitor. The evidence was plentiful. Sir Edward Baynton, the queen's Vice Chamberlain, reported in convoluted language, 'As for pastime in the queen's chamber, [there] was never more. If any of you that be now departed have any ladies that ye thought favoured you … I can no wit perceive the same by their dancing and pastime they do use here, but that other take place, as ever hath been the custom.'[23] Sir John Spelman, one of the crown's itinerant justices and observer at Anne's trial, noted 'all the evidence was of bawdry and lechery, so there was no such whore in the realm' as the queen.[24] Then there were Anne's appalling words about 'dead men's shoes'. What kind of woman would say words like that? And if one probed the queen's past reputation as a young lady of the court it was not hard to find or make up any number of lecherous stories, not the least being that the baby Elizabeth had been obviously conceived out of wedlock. The sixteenth-century conclusion was inescapable.

Is the twenty-first century therefore constrained to think likewise? Was Anne Boleyn actually guilty as condemned? Here the available evidence is so delicately balanced that it is impossible to offer firm judgement, Bernard says yes, Ives says no. Smeton's confession and Anne's conversation with Norris must be weighed against the fact that the government was unable to prove beyond doubt a single act of adultery as described in the various indictments. With one important exception all the victims in their scaffold addresses confessed they deserved to die. This was far more than the traditional Christian admission that all humans are sinners and in need of God's mercy and forgiveness.

Every sinner is subject to condemnation
Every man is a sinner. Ergo
Every man is subject to condemnation.

In different phrases and with different intensity they acknowledged their many, but never named, sins and used varying words to describe the extremity of the sinfulness. Smeton denied treason but went to his grave having declared his adultery with the queen and admitting that he was 'justly punished for his misdeeds' and 'deserved the death'. Weston used the word abomination to heighten his offence – 'I had thought to live in abomination yet this twenty or thirty years, and then to have made amend' – and he apologised so profusely to his wife to forgive him his offences and to pray for him that Bernard places him high on his list of potential bedmates for the queen. Norris said little but according to the *Spanish Chronicle* apologised to the king and said he deserved to die. Brereton avowed he 'deserved to die if it were a thousand deaths' but asked, 'the cause whereof I die judge ye not'. George Boleyn was the most loquacious and religious: 'I have known no man so evil, and to rehearse my sins openly, it were no pleasure to you to hear them, nor yet for me to rehearse them, for God knoweth all.' In another version of his speech he acknowledged 'he deserved a heavier punishment for his other sins, but not from the king, whom he had never offended'. He asked 'all the world forgiveness' but left it unclear whether this included his wife and her fatal accusation that he had slept with his sister.[25]

The great exception is Anne: she not only fervently and persistently avowed and swore to her innocence even while participating in the ritual of the mass but she also refused in her dying words to confess any guilt or declare she deserved death. This was absolutely exceptional and no other state traitor ever did so. There were excellent reasons to follow the prescribed death speech formula: execution by the axe could even at the last minute be replaced by the horror of burning at the stake or by the agony of mutilation by hanging, castration and disembowelment; children and wives could be persecuted for years in the future; and estates sequestered for generations. The recipe for death was carefully scripted: admit your guilt, acknowledge the justice of your trial and wish the king a long and happy life. Anne declared her willingness to die by the laws of the land but that is a world apart from saying you deserve to die. Edward Hall in *The Triumphant Reigne of Kyng Henry the VIII* reported her saying that 'if in my life I did ever offend the King's Grace, surely with my death I do now atone', and 'I submit to death with a good will'. The Portuguese version adds, 'I blame not my judges, nor any other manner of person, nor anything save the cruel law of the land by which I die,'[26] but not a word about guilt or deserving to die.

The conflicting evidence for guilt and innocence may be exquisitely balanced, but for Henry and the overwhelming majority of his subjects there could be no doubt or indecision. God had revealed the queen's sins, and she and all her paramours were guilty as charged. Eighteen years earlier Henry had felt that his conscience, when declaring his marriage to Katherine to be sinful and a violation of divine decree, was right 'not because so many said it' but because Henry, as a Christian and divine-right sovereign, knew 'the matter to be right'. Conscience, the king averred, 'was a private court, yet it is the high and supreme court for judgement or justice'. By the same impeccable logic he knew Anne to be a whore. His generation and even Thomas Cranmer, who had loved the lady, agreed, and the twenty-seven peers on her trial jury confirmed divine truth had spoken; there could be no further debate. Alas, the twenty-first century can no longer discern the voice of divinity and must leave the final judgement of guilt or innocence in doubt or to make-believe. Elizabeth I of England expressed much the same sentiment about her mother but in far briefer form when she wrote, 'The past cannot be cured.'

Bibliography

The Apocrypha, trans. Edgar Goodspeed, Modern Library edition, Random House (New York, 1959).

Bacon, Francis, *Works*, Vol. VI (London: 1826).

Bainton, R. H., *Here I Stand, A Life of Martin Luther* (New York, 1950).

Baldwin, William, *A Treatise of Morall Philosophie* (1547), ed. Robert H. Bowers (Florida, 1967).

Bernard, G. W., *Anne Boleyn: Fatal Attraction* (New Haven, 2011).

Burnet, Gilbert, *The History of the Reformation of the Church of England*, Vol. I (London, 1839).

Calendar of State Papers, Spanish, ed. M. A. S. Hume and Royall Tyler (London, 1862–1952).

Calendar of State Papers, Venetian, 9 vols, ed. R. Brown, *et al.* (London, 1864–98).

Cavendish, George, *Life and Death of Cardinal Wolsey in Two Early Tudor Lives*, eds Richard Sylvester and David Harding (New Haven, 1962).

Cranmer, Thomas, *Miscellaneous Writings and Letters*, ed. J. E. Cox (Cambridge, 1846).

De Carles, Lancelot, 'Histoire de Anne Boullant royne d'Angleterre' in Georges Ascoli, *La Grande-Bretagne devant l'opinion française* (Paris, 1929).

Duggan, Christopher, 'The Advent of Political Thought-Control in England: Seditious and Treasonable Speech, 1485–1547', unpublished PhD dissertation (Northwestern University, 1993).

'Ecclesiasticus' or 'The Wisom of Sirach', in Mathew, Thomas (trans.), Bible (London, 1537).

Elton, G. R., 'Thomas Cromwell' in *Encyclopaedia Britannica*, Vol. 6, pp. 799–800.

Elton, G. R., *The Tudor Constitution* (Cambridge, 1968).

Elyot, Thomas, *Of the Knowledge Which Maketh A Wise Man*, ed. Edwin J. Howard (Oxford & Ohio, 1946).

Elyot, Thomas, *The Book named the Governor*, ed. S. E. Lehmberg (New York, 1962).

Erasmus, Desiderius, *Opus Epistolarum*, ed. P. S. and H. M. Allen, 11 vols (Oxford, 1906–47).

Foxe, John, *Acts and Monuments*, ed. George Townsend, 8 vols (London, 1843–9).

Friedmann, Paul, *Anne Boleyn: A Chapter of English History*, 2 vols (London, 1884).

Froude, James A., *History of England from the Fall of Wolsey to the Defeat of the Spanish Armada*, 12 vols (New York, 1877).

Hall, Edward, *The Union of the Two Noble and Illustre Families of Lancastre & Yorke* (London, 1548).

Henry VIII, *Love Letters*, ed. H. Savage (London, 1949).

Henry VIII, *The Letters of King Henry VIII*, ed. Muriel St Clare Byrne (London, 1968).

Herbert, Edward Lord of Cherbury, *History of England under Henry VIII* (London, 1870).

Hume, M. A. S., *Chronicle of King Henry VIII* (London, 1889).

Ives, Eric, *The Life and Death of Anne Boleyn* (Oxford, 2005).

Letters and Papers, Foreign and Domestic, of the Reign of Henry VIII, ed. J. Gairdner and R. H. Brodie, 21 vols (London, 1862–1910).

Lovejoy, Arthur O., *The Great Chain of Being: A Study of an Idea* (Cambridge, Mass., 1936).

More, Thomas, *English Works* (1557), ed. W. E. Cambell and A. W. Reed, 2 vols (London, 1931).

Mulcaster, Richard, *The first Part of the Elementarie which entreateth chefelie of the right writing of our English Tung*, ed. E. T. Campagnac (Oxford, 1925).

Neale, John, *Queen Elizabeth I* (New York, 1957).

Nott, G. F., *The Works of Henry Howard, Earl of Surrey and of Sir Thomas Wyatt, the Elder*, Vol. II (London, 1815–6).

Parker, Matthew, *Correspondence*, ed. J. Bruce and T. Perowne (Cambridge, 1853).

Pickthorn, Kenneth, *Early Tudor Government: Henry VIII* (Cambridge, 1934).

Sander, Nicolas, *Rise and Growth of the Anglican Schism*, ed. D. Lewis (1877).

Scarisbrick, J. J., *Henry VIII* (Berkeley, 1968).

Shakespeare, William, *Troilus and Cressida*.

Smith, Lacey B., *Henry VIII: Mask of Royalty* (London, 1971).

Smith, Lacey B., *This Realm of England: 1399-1688* (Boston, 2001).

Smith, Lacey B., *Treason in Tudor England, Politics & Paranoia* (London, 2006).

Smith, Lacey B., *Tudor Prelates and Politics* (Princeton, 1953).

Spanish Chronicle, see Hume, M. A. S., *Chronicle of King Henry VIII*.

St German, Christopher, *Doctor and Student*, ed. T. Plucknett and J. Barton (1974).

Starkey, Thomas, *A Dialogue Between Reginald Pole and Thomas Lupset*, ed. Kathleen Burton (London, 1948).

State Papers during the Reign of Henry VIII, 11 vols. (London, 1830–52).

Strickland, Agnes, *Lives of the Queens of England*, Vol. II (London, 1852).

Strype, John, *Memorials of Thomas Cranmer*, 3 vols (Oxford, 1848).

Thomas, Keith, *Religion and the Decline of Magic* (New York, 1971).

Thomas, William, *The Pilgrim: a Dialogue on the Life and Actions of King Henry the Eighth*, ed. J. Froude (London, 1861).

Tillyard, E. M. W., *The Elizabethan World Picture* (New York, n.d.).

Tyndale, William, 'Obedience of a Christian Man' in H. Walter (ed.), *Doctrinal Treatise and Introductions to Different Portions of Scripture* (Cambridge, 1848).

Warnicke, Retha, M., *The Rise and Fall of Anne Boleyn: Family politics at the Court of Henry VIII* (Cambridge, 1991).

Weir, Alison, *The Lady in the Tower: The Fall of Anne Boleyn* (New York, 2010).

Wilson, Thomas, *The Arte of Rhetorique* (1553), ed. Robert Bowers (Florida, 1962).

Wriothesley, Charles, *A Chronicle of England*, ed. W. D. Hamilton, 2 vols (new series XI and XX, London, 1875, 1877).

Wyatt, George, *Papers*, ed. D. M. Loades (1968).

Notes

Full titles, names of editors and dates are given in the bibliography.

1 Setting the Stage

1. Ives, *Anne Boleyn*, p. 55.
2. Friedmann, *Anne Boleyn*, II, p. 312.

2 Early Life & Education

1. Warnicke, *Anne Boleyn*, p. 9.
2. Ives, *Anne Boleyn*, pp. 16–17.
3. Smith, *Treason in Tudor England*, p. 95.
4. *Ecclesiasticus*, 1:1, 3:1-2, 8:17-20, 9:10-12, 9:13-18, 11:29-30, 12:16-19.
5. Wilson, *The Art of Rhetorique*, fol. I (p. 13).
6. Smith, *Treason in Tudor England*, p. 86.
7. Ives, Anne Boleyn, p. 19.
8. *Ibid.*

3 Cultural & Religious Environment

1. Mulcaster, *The Elementarie*, p. 24.

2. E. M. W. Tillyard, *The Elizabethan World Picture* and Arthur Lovejoy, *The Great Chain of Being* are indispensable for the Tudor universe.

3. Shakespeare, *Troilus and Cressida*.

4. Elyot, *Governor*, p. 1.

5. Tillyard, *Elizabethan World*, p. 88.

6. Starkey, *Dialogue*, p. 45ff.

7. Cranmer, *Writings*, p. 235.

8. Elyot, *Of Knowledge*, p. 170.

9. Baldwin, *Morall Philosophie*, fol. 93 (p. 201).

10. *Ibid.*, fol. 157 (p. 329); *Treason in Tudor England*, p. 125.

11. Bacon, *Works*, VI, p. 747.

12. Smith, *Treason in Tudor England*, p. 128.

13. *Ibid.*, p. 129.

14. *Letters and Papers* (hereafter abbreviated as *L and P*), XIII (1), no. 1199 (2).

15. Thomas, *Religion and the Decline of Magic*, pp. 472, 476.

16. Smith, *Henry VIII*, p. 15.7.

17. *State Papers*, IX, p. 179.

18. Bainton, *Here I Stand*, p. 45.

19. More, *English Works*, pp. 207–8.

20. Foxe, *Acts and Monuments*, IV, p. 635.

4 The Court of Henry VIII

1. *Cal. S. P. Venetian*, 1527–33, p. 824.

2. De Carles, *Anne Boullant*, lines 62–8; Ives, *Anne Boleyn*, p. 44.

3. Thomas, *Pilgrim*, p. 70.

4. Ives, *Anne Boleyn*, p. 89.

5. Cavendish, *Wolsey*, p. 12.

6. *Ibid.*, pp. 32–5.

7. Ives, *Anne Boleyn*, pp. 72–80.

8. Henry VIII, *Love Letters*, pp. 32–4.

9. Ives, *Anne Boleyn*, pp. 85–7.

10. Henry VIII, *Love Letters*, pp. 34–6.

11. Ives, *Anne Boleyn*, pp. 84–92.

12. Bernard, *Anne Boleyn*, p. 31.

13. *Ibid.*

5 The King's Great Matter

1. Ives, *Anne Boleyn*, pp. 83–90.

2. Warnicke, *Rise and Fall*, p. 69.

3. *L and P*, IV, 6111; Smith, *Henry VIII*, p. 111.

4. Smith, *Henry VIII*, p. 112.

5. *Cal. S. P. Venetian*, II, 1287, p. 559; Smith, *Henry VIII*, p. 101.

6. Henry VIII, *Letters*, p. 78; Smith, *Henry VIII*, p. 104.

7. Smith, *Henry VIII*, p. 102.

8. Cranmer, *Writings*, pp. 84, 89, 106; Smith, *Henry VIII*, pp. 103–4.

9. Smith, *Henry VIII*, p. 108.

10. *L and P*, II, ii, 3163; Smith, *Henry VIII*, p. 110.

11. Cranmer, *Writings*, p. 88; Smith, *Henry VIII*, p. 111.

12. Henry VIII, *Letters*, p. 62; Smith, *Henry VIII*, p. 109.

13. *L and P*, VI, i, 775; Smith, *Henry VIII*, p. 116.

14. Henry VIII, *Letters*, p. 86; Smith, *Henry VIII*, p. 116.

15. *L and P*, X, 797; Bernard, *Anne Boleyn*, p. 106.

16. A rumour was circulated briefly after Katherine's death from natural causes that she had been poisoned by a mysterious substance sent from Italy by Gregory di Cosalo, the king's representative at the Vatican.

17. Cavendish, *Wolsey*, p. 38; Ives, *Anne Boleyn*, p. 103.

18. *L and P*, IV, ii, 4480; Bernard, *Anne Boleyn*, pp. 45–9.

19. *Cal. S. P. Spanish*, III, ii, no. 620, p. 887; Bernard, *Anne Boleyn*, p. 51.

20. Ives, *Anne Boleyn*, p. 128.

21. *Ibid.*, p. 129.

22. *Ibid.*, p. 135.

23. *L and P*, V, 105; Ives, *Anne Boleyn*, p. 138.

24. Ives, *Anne Boleyn*, p. 138.

25. *Ibid.*, p. 128.

26. *Ibid.*, pp. 132–9; Bernard, *Anne Boleyn*, p. 53–6.

27. Bernard, *Anne Boleyn*, pp. 54–6.

28. St German, *Doctor and Student*, pp. 315, 327; Ives, *Anne Boleyn*, p. 149.

29. Elton, *Tudor Constitution*, p. 346.

30. Ives, *Anne Boleyn*, p. 171.

31. *Ibid.*, pp. 168–70.

32. Bernard, Ives, and Warnicke have long descriptions of the Coronation taken mainly from Edward Hall, *Union of Two Noble Families*, pp. 798–805.

33. Smith, *This Realm of England*, pp. 121–2.

6 Married to a King

1. Ives, *Anne Boleyn*, p. 260.

2. *Ibid.*

3. *Ibid.*, p. 264.

4. *Ibid.*, p. 269.

5. *Ibid.*, p. 280.

6. *Ibid.*, p. 272.

7. *Ibid.*, p. 280.

8. Bernard, *Anne Boleyn*, p. 93.

9. Warnicke, *Rise and Fall*, pp. 152, 162.

10. Foxe, *Acts and Monuments*, V, p. 175.

11. *L and P*, X, 615 (4); Bernard, *Anne Boleyn*, pp. 116–23.

12. Parker, *Correspondence*, IX, p. 9.

13. Warnicke, *Rise and Fall*, p. 162.

14. Ives, *Anne Boleyn*, p. 201.

15. Smith, *Tudor Prelates*, pp. 100–1.

16. Cavendish, *Wolsey*, p. 119.

17. Tyndale, *Works*, I, p. 240; Ives, *Anne Boleyn*, p. 133.

18. Elton, *Tudor Constitution*, 177, pp. 344–49.

19. *Ibid.*, pp. 230–1; Smith, *Realm of England*, p. 127.

20. *Ibid.*, 180, p. 355.

21. Duggan, 'Advent of Political Thought-Control', pp. 215, 217, 261.

22. Elton, *Tudor Constitution*, 30, p. 62–3.

23. Smith, *Realm of England*, p. 123.

24. Foxe, *Acts and Monuments*, VIII, p. 33.

25. Elton, *Tudor Constitution*, pp. 6–12; Pickthorn, *Tudor Government*, pp. 234–5.

26. Smith, *Realm of England*, p. 122.

27. Smith, *Realm of England*, p. 122–3.

28. *L and P*, IX, 873; Ives, *Anne Boleyn*, p. 198.

29. *L and P*, VII, 871.

30. *Ibid.*, VII, 296; Bernard, *Anne Boleyn*, p. 82.

31. Warnicke, *Rise and Fall*, p. 172.

32. Bernard, *Anne Boleyn*, p. 90.

33. Ives, *Anne Boleyn*, p. 192.

34. *Ibid.*, p. 194.

7 Miscarriage to Execution – Four Versions

1. Ives, Anne Boleyn, p. 15; Friedmann, p. 29.

2. *L and P*, X, 199; Ives, *Anne Boleyn*, pp. 297–8.

3. Ives, *Anne Boleyn*, p. 302.

4. *L and P*, X, 601; Ives, *Anne Boleyn*, p. 304.

5. Ives, *Anne Boleyn*, p. 335.

6. *Ibid.*, pp. 336, 347.

7. *Spanish Chronicle*, p. 55–9; Ives, *Anne Boleyn*, p. 329.

8. De Carles, *Anne Boullant*, lines 437–44; Ives, *Anne Boleyn*, pp. 333–34.

9. Wriothesley, *Chronicle*, I, pp. 37–8; Ives, *Anne Boleyn*, p. 340.

10. De Carles, *Anne Boullant*, lines 1002–12; Ives, *Anne Boleyn*, p. 341.

11. *Union of Two Noble Families*, p. 819; Ives, *Anne Boleyn*, pp. 357–8.

12. Bernard, *Anne Boleyn*, p. 129.

13. *Ibid.*, p. 131.

14. *Ibid.*

15. *Ibid.*, p. 134.

16. *Ibid.*, p. 132.

17. *Ibid.*, p. 140.

18. *Ibid.*, p. 141.

19. *Ibid.*, p. 146.

20. *Ibid.*, p. 147.

21. *Ibid.*, pp. 147–8.

22. *L and P*, X, 1069, 908; Bernard, *Anne Boleyn*, p. 150.

23. Bernard, *Anne Boleyn*, p. 152.

24. *Ibid.*, pp. 158–60.

25. *L and P*, X, 793; Bernard, *Anne Boleyn*, p. 163.

26. Bernard, *Anne Boleyn*, p. 165

27. *Ibid.*, p. 168.

28. *Ibid.*, p. 181.

29. *Ibid.*, p. 192.

30. See earlier in this book, pages 44–45.

31. Warnicke, *Rise and Fall*, pp. 3–4.

32. *Ibid.*, p. 207.

33. *Ibid.*, p. 235.

34. Strype, *Memorials of Thomas Cranmer*, I, p. 389.

35. Weir, *Lady in the Tower*, p. 30.

36. *Ibid.*, p. 10.

37. *Ibid.*, pp. 11–12.

38. *Ibid.*, pp. 19–20.

39. *Ibid.*, p. 38.

40. *Ibid.*, p. 57.

41. *Ibid.*, p. 69.

42. *Ibid.*, p. 72.

43. *Ibid.*, pp. 86–7.

44. *Ibid.*, pp. 103–12.

45. *Ibid.*, pp. 114–9, 125.

46. Strype, *Memorials of Thomas Cranmer*, I, p. 390.

47. Hume, *Spanish Chronicle*, pp. 68–9.

48. Weir, *Lady in the Tower*, pp. 179–80.

49. *Ibid.*, p. 203.

50. *Ibid.*, p. 225.

51. *Ibid.*, p. 230.

52. *Ibid.*, p. 235.

53. *Ibid.*, P. 238.

54. *Ibid.*, p. 248

55. *Ibid.*, p. 254.

56. *Ibid.*, p. 282. This is the version of a Portuguese bystander and is modelled on Edward Hall, *Union of Two Noble Families*.

57. Weir, *Lady in the Tower*, p. 290.

8 The King's Mind

1. Bernard, *Anne Boleyn*, p. 146.

2. G. R. Elton, *Encyclopaedia Britannica*, VI, 'Thomas Cromwell', p. 800.

3. Strype, *Memorials of Thomas Cranmer*, I, pp. 389–90.

4. Weir, *Lady in the Tower*, pp. 69, 70.

5. *L and P*, X, 1069; Ives, *Anne Boleyn*, p. 318.

6. *L and P*, II, 1991, p. 580.

7. Smith, *Henry VIII*, p. 88.

8. *Ibid.*, pp. 89–90.

9. Weir, *Lady in the Tower*, p. 97.

10. *State Papers* VI, 114, p. 417.

11. Smith, *Henry VIII*, p. 95.

12. *Ibid.*, pp. 95–96.

13. Erasmus, *Opus Epistolarum*, VIII, ep. 2143, p. 129; Smith, *Henry VIII*, p. 96.

14. Smith, *Henry VIII*, p. 53.

15. *Ibid.*, p. 50.

16. *L and P*, XIV, i, 237; Smith, *Henry VIII*, p. 57.

17. *Ibid.*, p. 104.

18. Weir, *Lady in the Tower*, p. 68.

19. Smith, *Henry VIII*, p. 104.

20. Henry VIII, *Letters*, p. 68.

21. Weir, *Lady in the Tower*, pp. 176, 184.

22. Strype, *Memorials of Thomas Cranmer*, I, pp. 289–90; Weir, *Lady in the Tower*, p. 154.

23. Bernard, *Anne Boleyn*, pp. 185–6.

24. Ives, *Anne Boleyn*, p. 345.

25. Weir, *Lady in the Tower*, pp. 254–5.

26. *Ibid.*, pp. 281–2.

List of Illustrations

Also available from Amberley Publishing

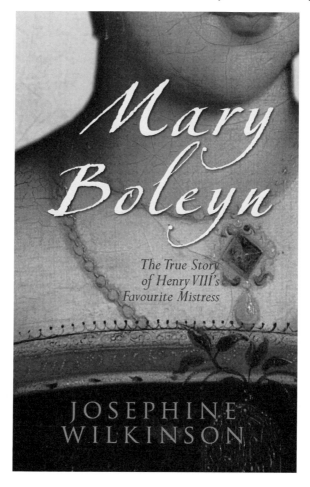

The scandalous true story of Mary Boleyn, infamous sister of Anne, and mistress of Henry VIII

Mary Boleyn, 'the infamous other Boleyn girl', began her court career as the mistress of the king of France. François I of France would later call her 'The Great Prostitute' and the slur stuck. The bête-noir of her family, Mary was married off to a minor courtier but it was not long before she caught the eye of Henry VIII and a new affair began.

Mary would emerge the sole survivor of a family torn apart by lust and ambition, and it is in Mary and her progeny that the Boleyn legacy rests.

£9.99 Paperback
22 illustrations (10 colour)
224 pages
978-1-84868-525-3

Available from all good bookshops or to order direct
Please call **01453–847–800**
www.amberleybooks.com

Also available from Amberley Publishing

The Young Queen To Be

Anne Boleyn

JOSEPHINE WILKINSON

'Based on meticulous research & hard evidence... highly recommended'
THEANNEBOLEYNFILES.COM

The story of Anne Boleyn's early life, told in detail for the first time

Anne Boleyn is perhaps the most engaging of Henry VIII's Queens. But before Henry came into her life
Anne Boleyn had already wandered down love's winding path. She had learned its twists and turns during
her youth spent at the courts of the Low Countries and France, where she had been sent as a result of her
scandalous behaviour with her father's butler and chaplain. Here her education had been directed by two of
the strongest women of the age – and one of the weakest.

£9.99 Paperback
34 illustrations (19 colour)
208 pages
978-1-4456-0395-7

Available from all good bookshops or to order direct
Please call **01453-847-800**
www.amberleybooks.com

Also available from Amberley Publishing

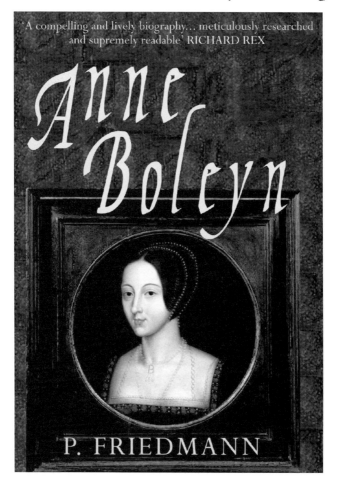

The classic biography of the most engaging of Henry VIII's wives

'Friedmann has an unparalleled mastery of the detail of his subject, which he weaves into a compelling and lively narrative. A meticulously researched and supremely readable classic of Tudor biography'
DR RICHARD REX, author of *Henry VIII: Tudor Tyrant* & *The Tudors*.

'The first scholarly biography' JENNY UGLOW, *THE FINANCIAL TIMES*

Friedmann charts the rise and fall of Anne Boleyn, from her origins as the daughter of a gifted and ambitious courtier, her elevation to the greatest heights a woman could reach, to her tragic fall and execution, the victim of the man who had once loved her, and who had altered the course of his country's history forever in order to have her.

£20 Hardback
47 illustrations (20 colour)
352 pages
978-1-84868-827-8

Available from all good bookshops or to order direct
Please call **01453-847-800**
www.amberleybooks.com

Also available from Amberley Publishing

The tragic love affair that changed English history forever

'Meticulously researched and a great read' *THEANNEBOLEYNFILES.COM*

Anne Boleyn was the most controversial and scandalous woman ever to sit on the throne of England. From her early days at the imposing Hever Castle in Kent, to the glittering courts of Paris and London, Anne caused a stir wherever she went. Alluring but not beautiful, Anne's wit and poise won her numerous admirers at the English court, and caught the roving eye of King Henry.

Their love affair was as extreme as it was deadly, from Henry's 'mine own sweetheart' to 'cursed and poisoning whore' her fall from grace was total.

£9.99 Paperback
47 illustrations (26 colour)
264 pages
978-1-84868-514-7

Available from all good bookshops or to order direct
Please call **01453-847-800**
www.amberleybooks.com

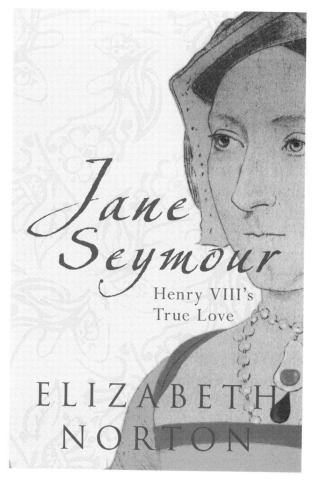

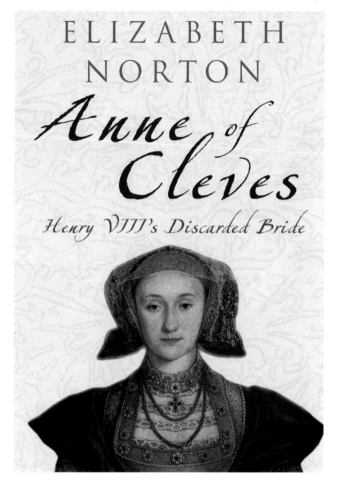

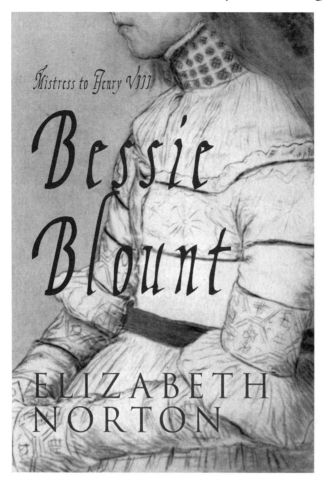

Also available from Amberley Publishing

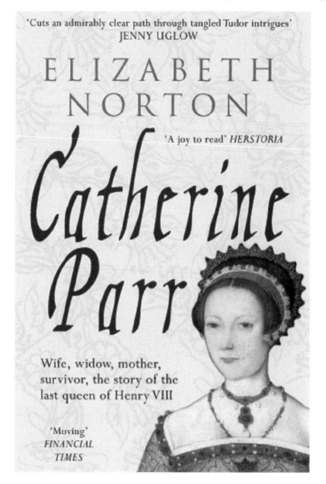

'Cuts an admirably clear path through tangled Tudor intrigues'
JENNY UGLOW

ELIZABETH NORTON

'A joy to read' HERSTORIA

Catherine Parr

Wife, widow, mother, survivor, the story of the last queen of Henry VIII

'Moving'
FINANCIAL TIMES

Wife, widow, mother, survivor, the story of the last queen of Henry VIII

'Scintillating' *THE FINANCIAL TIMES*
'Norton cuts an admirably clear path through the tangled Tudor intrigues' *JENNY UGLOW*
'Wonderful, an excellent book, a joy to read' *HERSTORIA*

The sixth wife of Henry VIII was also the most married queen of England, outliving three husbands before finally marrying for love. Catherine Parr was enjoying her freedom after her first two arranged marriages when she caught the attention of the elderly Henry VIII. She was the most reluctant of all Henry's wives, offering to become his mistress rather than submit herself to the dangers of becoming Henry's queen. This only served to increase Henry's enthusiasm for the young widow and Catherine was forced to abandon her lover for the decrepit king.

£9.99 Paperback
49 illustrations (39 colour)
304 pages
978-1-4456-0383-4

Available from all good bookshops or to order direct
Please call **01453-847-800**
www.amberleybooks.com

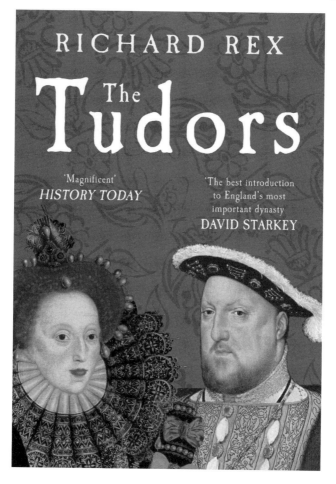

Also available from Amberley Publishing

The complete letters, dispatches and chronicles that tell the real story of Anne Boleyn

'A very useful compilation of source material on Anne Boleyn' ALISON WEIR

Through the chronicles, letters and dispatches written by both Anne and her contemporaries, it is possible to see her life and thoughts as she struggled to become queen of England, ultimately ending her life on the scaffold. Only through the original sources is it truly possible to evaluate the real Anne. George Wyatt's *Life of Queen Anne* provided the first detailed account of the queen, based on the testimony of those that knew her. The poems of Anne's supposed lover, Thomas Wyatt, as well as accounts such as Cavendish's *Life of Wolsey* also give details of her life, as do the hostile dispatches of the Imperial Ambassador, Eustace Chapuys and the later works of the slanderous Nicholas Slander and Nicholas Harpsfield. Henry VIII's love letters and many of Anne's own letters survive, providing an insight into the love affair that changed England forever. The reports on Anne's conduct in the Tower of London show the queen's shock and despair when she realised that she was to die. Collected together for the first time, these and other sources make it possible to view the real Anne Boleyn through her own words and those of her contemporaries.

£25 Hardback
45 illustrations
352 pages
978-1-4456-0043-7

Available from all good bookshops or to order direct
Please call **01453-847-800**
www.amberleybooks.com

Also available from Amberley Publishing

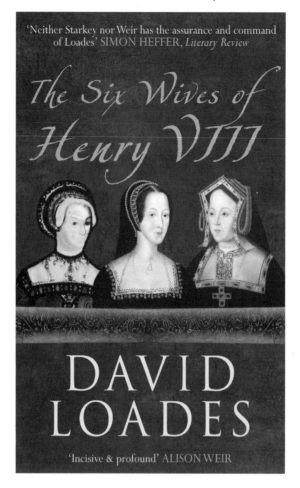

The marital ups and downs of England's most infamous king

'Neither Starkey nor Weir has the assurance and command of Loades'
SIMON HEFFER, LITERARY REVIEW

'Incisive and profound... I warmly recommend this book' ALISON WEIR

The story of Henry VIII and his six wives has passed from history into legend – taught in the cradle as a cautionary tale and remembered in adulthood as an object lesson in the dangers of marrying into royalty. The true story behind the legend, however, remains obscure to most people, whoe knowledge of the affair begins and ends with the aide memoire 'Divorced, executed, died, divorce, executed, survived'.

£9.99 Paperback
55 illustrations (31 colour)
224 pages
978-1-4456-004-9

Available from all good bookshops or to order direct
Please call **01453-847-800**
www.amberleybooks.com

Also available from Amberley Publishing

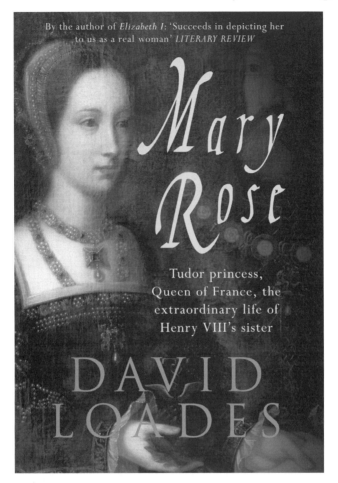

Tudor Princess, Queen of France, the scandalous life of Henry VIII's sister

'Mary, queen of hearts' *HISTORY TODAY*

'A paradise... tall, slender, grey-eyed, possessing an extreme pallor'. The contemporary view of Henry VIII's younger sister, Princess Mary Rose as one of the most beautiful princesses in Europe, was an arresting one. Glorious to behold, this Tudor Princess with her red hair flowing loose to her waist, was also impossible for Henry to control.

David Loades' biography, the first for almost 50 years brings the princess alive once more. Of all Tudor women, this queen of France and later Duchess of Suffolk remains an elusive, enigmatic figure.

£20 Hardback
40 illustrations (20 colour)
272 pages
978-1-4456-0622-4

Available from all good bookshops or to order direct
Please call **01453-847-800**
www.amberleybooks.com

Forthcoming February 2013 from Amberley Publishing

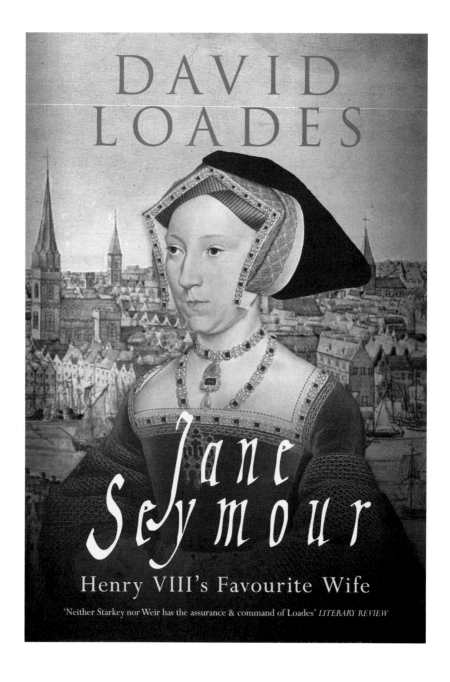

DAVID LOADES

Jane Seymour

Henry VIII's Favourite Wife

'Neither Starkey nor Weir has the assurance & command of Loades' *LITERARY REVIEW*

Available from all good bookshops or to order direct
Please call **01453–847–800**
www.amberleybooks.com

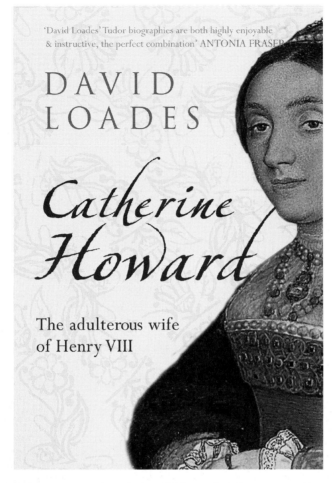

Also available from Amberley Publishing

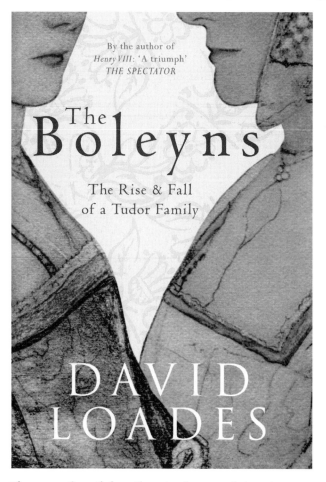

By the author of
Henry VIII: 'A triumph'
THE SPECTATOR

The
Boleyns

The Rise & Fall
of a Tudor Family

DAVID
LOADES

*A magnificent tale of family rivalry and intrigue set against
Henry VIII's court*

The fall of Anne Boleyn and her brother George is the classic drama of the Tudor era. The Boleyns had long been an influential English family. Sir Edward Boleyn had been Lord Mayor of London. His grandson, Sir Thomas had inherited wealth and position, and through the sexual adventures of his daughters, Mary and Anne, ascended to the peak of influence at court. The three Boleyn children formed a faction of their own, making many enemies: and when those enemies secured Henry VIII's ear, they brought down the entire family in blood and disgrace.

£10.99 Paperback
34 illustrations (24 colour)
312 pages
978-1-4456-0304-9

Available from all good bookshops or to order direct
Please call **01453-847-800**
www.amberleybooks.com

Also available from Amberley Publishing

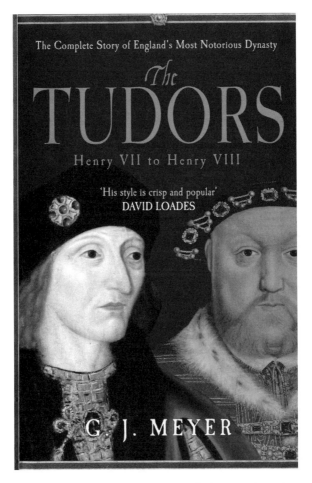

A superb narrative history of the Tudor dynasty

In 1485, young Henry Tudor, whose claim to the throne was so weak as to be almost laughable, crossed the English Channel from France at the head of a ragtag little army and took the crown from the family that had ruled England for almost four hundred years. Half a century later his son, Henry VIII, desperate to rid himself of his first wife in order to marry a second, launched a reign of terror aimed at taking powers no previous monarch had even dreamed of possessing. In the process he plunged his kingdom into generations of division and disorder, creating a legacy of blood and betrayal that would blight the lives of his children and the destiny of his country.

£12.99 Paperback
72 illustrations (54 colour)
384 pages
978-1-4456-0143-4

Available from all good bookshops or to order direct
Please call **01453-847-800**
www.amberleybooks.com

Also available from Amberley Publishing

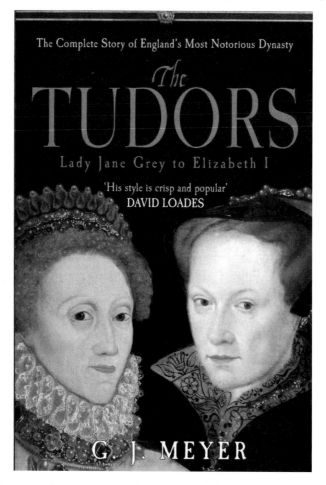

A superb narrative history of the Tudor dynasty

For the first time in decades, a fresh look at the fabled Tudor dynasty, comprising some of the most enigmatic figures ever to rule England. Acclaimed historian G. J. Meyer reveals the flesh-and-bone reality in all its wild excess. The boy king Edward VI, a fervent believer in reforming the English church, died before bringing to fruition his dream of a second English Reformation. Mary I, the disgraced daughter of Catherine of Aragon, tried and failed to reestablish the Catholic Church and produce an heir. And finally came Elizabeth I, who devoted her life to creating an image of herself as Gloriana the Virgin Queen but, behind that mask, sacrificed all chance of personal happiness in order to survive. *The Tudors* weaves together all the sinners and saints, the tragedies and triumphs, the high dreams and dark crimes, that reveal the Tudor era to be, in its enthralling, notorious truth, as momentous and as fascinating as the fictions audiences have come to love.

£12.99 Paperback
53 illustrations (15 colour)
352 pages
978-1-4456-0144-1

Available from all good bookshops or to order direct
Please call **01453-847-800**
www.amberleybooks.com

Also available from Amberley Publishing

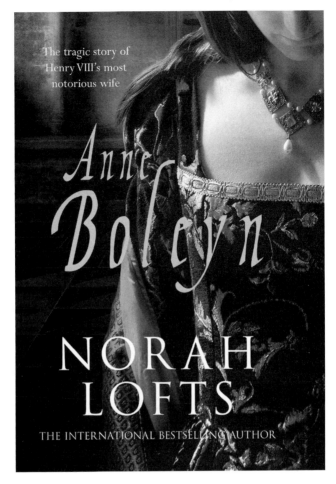

The tragic story of Henry VIII's most notorious wife

Also available from Amberley Publishing

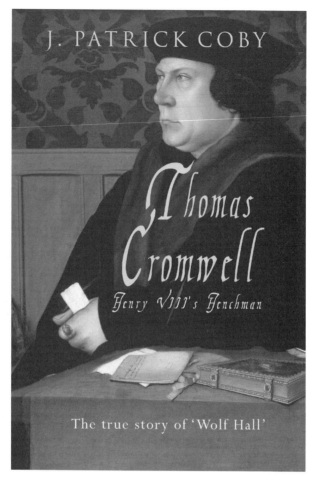

The real story of 'Wolf Hall'

Thomas Cromwell, chief architect of the English Reformation served as chief minister of Henry VIII from 1531 to 1540, the most tumultuous period in Henry's thirty-seven-year reign. Many of the momentous events of the 1530s are attributed to Cromwell's agency, the Reformation, the dissolution of the monasteries and the fall of Henry's second wife, the bewitching Anne Boleyn.

Cromwell has been the subject of close and continuous attention for the last half century, with positive appraisal of his work and achievements by historians, this new biography shows the true face of a Machiavellian Tudor statesmans of no equal.

£20 Hardback
30 illustrations (10 col)
292 pages
978-1-4456-0775-7

Available from all good bookshops or to order direct
Please call **01453-847-800**
www.amberleybooks.com

Also available from Amberley Publishing

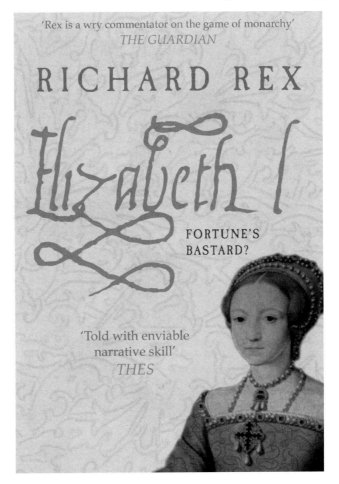

An accessible biography of Elizabeth I by a leading Tudor expert

Richard Rex highlights the vivid and contrary personality of a Queen who could both baffle and bedazzle her subjects, her courtiers, and her rivals: at one moment flirting outrageously with a favourite or courting some foreign prince, and at another vowing perpetual virginity; at one time agonising over the execution of her cousin, Mary Queen of Scots, then ordering the slaughter of hundreds of poor men after a half-cock rebellion. Too many biographies of Elizabeth merely perpetuate the flattery she enjoyed from her courtiers, this biography also reflects more critical voices, such as those of the Irish, the Catholics and those who lived on the wrong side of the emerging North/South divide. To them she showed a different face.

£9.99 Paperback
75 illustrations
192 pages
978-1-84868-423-2

Available from all good bookshops or to order direct
Please call **01453-847-800**
www.amberleybooks.com

Also available from Amberley Publishing

An accessible biography of Henry VIII by one of the country's leading Tudor experts

The future Henry VIII was born on 29 June 1491, the second son of Henry VII and Elizabeth of York. This talented, athletic and temperamental man might have proved something of a handful to his elder brother, Prince Arthur, the firstborn, had he survived to wear the crown. But Henry's life was changed forever when Arthur died in 1502 and the course of English history took a very unexpected turn...

£9.99 Paperback
81 illustrations (30 colour)
192 pages
978-1-84868-098-2

Available from all good bookshops or to order direct
Please call **01453-847-800**
www.amberleybooks.com

Also available from Amberley Publishing

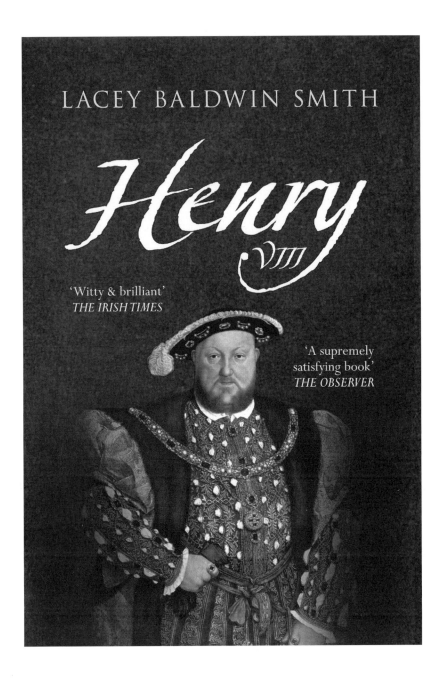

Available from all good bookshops or to order direct
Please call **01453–847–800**
www.amberleybooks.com

Also available from Amberley Publishing

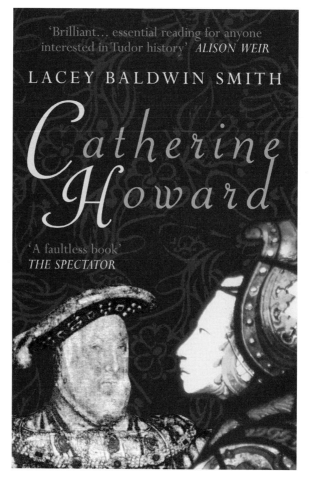

A biography of Henry VIII's fifth wife, beheaded for playing Henry at his own game – adultery

'Brilliant... essential reading for anyone interested in Tudor history' ALISON WEIR

'A faultless book' *THE SPECTATOR*

'Lacey Baldwin Smith has so excellently caught the atmosphere of the Tudor age' *THE OBSERVER*

£9.99 Paperback
25 colour illustrations
288 pages
978-1-84868-521-5

Available from all good bookshops or to order direct
Please call **01453-847-800**
www.amberleybooks.com

Index